Basic is Beautiful

Margaret Hebblethwaite was born in London in 1951 and read theology and philosophy at Oxford, with further studies at the Gregorian University in Rome. She has been involved in a wide variety of lay ministries, including prison chaplaincy work, spiritual direction and parish work on the Blackbird Leys estate in Oxford. She has visited base communities in Nicaragua, El Salvador and Brazil, and has worked with José Marins and his team, giving workshops in Birmingham on basic Christian community. Her books include *Motherhood and God* and *Finding God in All Things*. She is assistant editor at the Catholic weekly, *The Tablet*.

BASIC IS BEAUTIFUL

Basic Ecclesial Communities
from Third World to First World

Margaret Hebblethwaite

Fount
An Imprint of HarperCollins*Publishers*

Fount Paperbacks is an Imprint of
HarperCollins*Religious*
Part of HarperCollins*Publishers*
77–85 Fulham Palace Road, London w6 8jb

First published in Great Britain
in 1993 by Fount Paperbacks

1 3 5 7 9 10 8 6 4 2

A catalogue record for this book is
available from the British Library

ISBN 0 00 627470 6

Set in Linotron Bembo by
Rowland Phototypesetting Ltd
Bury St Edmunds, Suffolk

Printed and bound in Great Britain by
HarperCollinsManufacturing Glasgow

What is happening in Latin American Christian communities is part of God's calling us, in the North, to conversion.

(Henri Nouwen, in his introduction to *We Drink from our Own Wells*, by Gustavo Gutiérrez)

I guess or predict that the Basic Christian Communities or *comunidades de base* will prove to be *the* major powerful influence in the Church of the future. I predict they will affect the whole Church as deeply as the growth of the monastic orders, the Benedictines for example, from the fifth century to the Middle Ages; or the Jesuits and the other apostolic orders from the sixteenth to the present century; or the evolution of the Protestant Churches over the recent centuries.

I foresee the Church will form a consensus to promote the growth of the Basic Christian Communities, and this decision will be as important for the life of the Church as the decision made by the Council of Jerusalem to open the Church to the Gentiles on the Gentiles' terms.

(Bishop Julio X. Labayen of the Philippines, in an address given to the 25th anniversary of the Dutch Bishops' Lenten Campaign, 1985)

CONTENTS

A PERSONAL INTRODUCTION

I am often asked how I became interested in basic Christian communities. For me, as for every Catholic who is asked the question, the roots can be traced back to the Second Vatican Council, and the period of ferment and renewal that great event stimulated. When the Council came to an end in 1965 I was in my idealistic teens, and the Holy Spirit seemed to be blowing through the cobwebbed corridors of the Church in great blasts. Each little experiment in worship or Church organization opened up a new door to understanding the original meaning of the Christian tradition. There was a sense that the newness of the early Church was with us again, and that we could forge our future from first principles.

But like many others, I soon became frustrated by the slow pace of change. By the late sixties, everything seemed to be put on hold, and under a succession of popes, hopes of progress slowly faded into a painful realization that we had rather reverted to an era of "restoration". None the less, there had been a glimpse of a new Church, and the memory of it could not be erased. And so, when at last I heard of basic Christian communities, it was like finding a map of buried treasure. We might not yet have reached the right place to dig, but given the map, we know the treasure is there to be found.

If the Vatican Council was the remote preparation for my interest in basic Christian communities, the more immediate spur was my own search for somewhere to go to mass on Sunday. Disappointed by the missed opportunities of parish liturgies, I had wandered around restlessly in my teens and early twenties. Then I settled down in a congregation which was not a parish, but centred around a Sunday mass in the chapel of a religious community. Many "refugees" from parishes came here to worship each week, in search of a more lively liturgy and a more critical approach to Catholicism.

But as my involvement in this congregation grew, so too did my perception of certain internal contradictions. Though democracy and collaboration were loudly proclaimed, it was taken as impolite to question whether they were actually present. All the preaching, teaching and decision-making appeared in practice to remain in the hands of the clergy, so that given the rich resources of this rather unusual, self-selecting congregation, there was even more waste of talent here than in the parish churches. I became involved in an attempt to change the balance of responsibilities, expanding the role of the laity in a number of areas. But my meddling was not appreciated by the clergy, whose most frequent objection was to say, "We are not a parish". I was naïve enough to be sincerely baffled. "Of course we are not a parish," I would answer, "that is why we all come here, all of us refugees from parishes, because we want something different from the parish. Being not-a-parish gives us more freedom to do new things, not less . . ." But I found I was talking to myself.

After I had left this particular congregation and was once more wandering an ecclesial desert in search of a Christian homeland, the question remained with me. What does it mean, to be a Christian worshipping community which is not a parish? Or, to look at it from the other side, what does it mean to be a parish? What is and is not appropriate to those two sorts of ecclesial groups? Somewhere I had heard that in Latin America there were groups called base communities, which were not parishes. Perhaps they held a clue to our own situation. Or then again, perhaps they did not. Perhaps they were only a phenomenon for Latin America. They slipped once more from my mind.

For a year or two I did not bother to investigate further. Then one day I saw a book on a stall called *Ecclesiogenesis: The Base Communities Re-invent the Church*. It was by the famous Brazilian liberation theologian, Leonardo Boff, and the cover showed a primitive painting of a group seated in a circle and Jesus in the midst. I bought it and began to read. I had not reached the end of the first page before I knew that I was onto something very important indeed.

It would be simplistic and would betray the lack of a sense of history
to conceive of the basic church communities as a purely contingent,
transitory phenomenon . . . . Theologically they signify a new ecclesiological experience, a renaissance of very church, and hence an action
of the Spirit on the horizon of the matters urgent for our time.

If base communities were to be such a lasting phenomenon and of
such universal significance, I thought, they must be for all the
Church, and that meant for the first-world Church as well. By the
second page I was learning that

Perhaps we are now in a phase of the emergence of a new institutional
type of church. Our situation will have to be understood in the light
of the Holy Spirit. We must conquer our mental resistance, modify
our church habits, and stay open. Otherwise we may smother the
Spirit.

So basic Christian communities were not just another possible structure – they were the rebirth of the Church, the remaking of the
Church into something much closer to what it was supposed to be.
It is difficult to describe my excitement. If this were true, then it
would be worth the work of a lifetime helping this new way of being
Church to be born in more places. It might be slow work, but ahead
of us was the prophetic voice of those who had already, in their own
nations, begun to experience the fruit of "ecclesiogenesis" – the birth
of the Church.

Many of the issues I had encountered in my own experience were
addressed in Boff's work. Clericalism was indeed one of the biggest
obstacles requiring transformation. But there were also other challenges that stretched my vision. A major message to take on board
was the option for the poor. A renewed ecclesial community could
not just be for hyper-critical intellectuals, fed up with being talked
down to by a clergy who would not share their power. My frustration, as a theologically-educated, middle-class, white European, was
only a tiny part of the picture. Where were the poor in my thinking?
How could this new vision of Church reach the simple, ordinary
people? And not just reach them, as though as an after-thought, but
begin from where they were?

Over the next years I tried to live out the option for the poor in a number of ways. I worked for a couple of years on the chaplaincy team of a young persons' prison. From that I experienced the huge gap between the approaches of patronage and solidarity, between doing-for and being-with the marginalized. I also learned that Christian community takes time: every three or four months there was a change of prisoners, and the work that was just beginning had to start again.

I became involved in justice and peace work, both at home and overseas. From that I learned that there was a real spirit of discovery and celebration, among people both at home and abroad, who were together sharing the new perspectives of liberation. The Catholic Church was a wonderful channel for communication – not only of grassroots information about the forgotten poor, but also of everything that was most creative and alive in the Church today.

I began a Lent group in my own, socially-mixed locality, trying to explore the possibilities of a basic Christian community that was local and had very loose links with the Catholic parish. I put leaflets through doors of the lapsed Catholics (with the help of addresses from the parish priest) and through all the doors in the most run-down streets. The idea was to target primarily those who were in most need of basic Christian community, but I also made clear the invitation was open to all. I also put notices up in post offices and pubs: the post-office cards were quite effective, and brought in quite a few people I had never met before. But on the whole the people who came were already very active as Christians, mostly from other churches and mostly from outside the immediate area. They were a great bunch of people, but not a grassroots local community ready to rediscover the Gospel.

What really emerged was a prayer group, not a base community. From it I learned that the word of God could indeed come alive in the front room of an ordinary house in a way it never did in church. But I also learned that in our society the people who respond most quickly to an invitation mentioning basic Christian community, are those who need it least – the confident and the committed. A long, painstaking period of befriending is needed before the marginalized or the disillusioned will venture out. The poor could never be gathered together by leafletting, only by personal contact.

The group asked to continue after Easter, and it lasted until the summer. But I found that when I tried to phase out my leadership role, so that the meetings would go on happening when I was away or too busy to do the preparation for the evening, the group fizzled out and I did not then attempt to keep it going. I no longer felt the prayer group wanted to take the leap of transformation into basic Christian community.

Another major, creative influence in my exploration came from the team of José Marins, Carolee Chanona and Teolide Trevisan, who, at about the time of my own searchings, began to visit England each year with their basic Christian community workshops. Marins and Teo come from Brazil, and Carolee from the little country of Belize, in Central America. The team has been following the process of basic ecclesial communities for the last twenty or so years: giving workshops, helping in evaluation, accompanying and animating, not only throughout Latin America but also in the United States, Australia, Ireland, Portugal, the Caribbean, Africa, Asia . . . in fact, all over the world. I recognized in their workshops a voice and a message that the first world badly needed to hear, but one that would require some working out for our context. I became part of these workshops year after year, first as a participant, later as a local team member.

The next stage on my journey was to become part of the worshipping community on a council housing estate, where I became involved in parish planning and liturgy. From that I learned that however shy and diffident the people may be at first, once they take you into their hearts they are appreciative and solid friends. I became convinced that the work of transformation was possible, and it would be welcomed and appreciated, but it would take a long time and involve an enormous amount of work. The key to everything was the slow process of getting to know individuals in their homes.

I also began to feel that only the priest was effectively in a position to initiate this slow transformation in a parish. Lay team members would also be necessary but, until the priest caught the bug of base community, the work would be at a very preliminary level. Perhaps, after all, the most useful contribution I could make to base-community building as a laywoman was to reach clergy and pastoral agents, of all types and denominations, by writing a book.

Eventually I got together enough funds to visit some real-life,

Latin American base communities in Nicaragua, El Salvador and Brazil, and to attend the Seventh Interecclesial Assembly of Basic Ecclesial Communities at Duque de Caxias. By now there was a sense of coming home. I found nothing that I had not already been led to expect from my reading, but if there was one message that struck me more deeply than before it was this: Basic Christian community is something very, very ordinary. Simple, humble Christians in Central America are just like simple, humble Christians in Britain. An elusive dream and a romantic ideal had become attainable, down-to-earth and obvious.

There was also a deep conviction that it was not enough to go there as though that were the place I would rather be. To find a base community for oneself by going abroad (even supposing that had been possible for me, which it was not) would be an individualistic sort of solution, and would leave the rest of the Church untouched. For that reason it would be a solution that was directly contrary to the very principles of base community, which are anti-individualistic and in favour of jointly seeking common solutions.

If we are serious about the value of what the Latin American base communities were doing, then we have to help our own people find the way. Going to learn from the third world is one thing; shrugging our shoulders about the Church in our own country is another. Latin America does not need our expertise to build their Church: we need their expertise to build ours.

It will be evident that it has taken me some time to work out what base community means, in a sense that could be applied also to the first world. The answers I have come up with in the end are by no means a universally accepted orthodoxy, and not everyone would agree with all the points of my analysis. For some, a base community is by definition composed solely of the poor, so this is only a new way of being Church for some sections of society, not for everyone. For others, a base community is by definition something that happens in Latin America, so any attempt towards base community in the first world is an attempt to transplant a foreign product. For others again, a base community is by definition free of any hierarchy, so that where a base community still turns to the priest for the eucharist it has not yet lived up to the logic of its calling. For others yet again, a base community is by definition whatever kind of small group grows up naturally among the Christians in a particular culture, so that almost any kind of group can be called a basic Christian community.

For my own part, I hold none of those positions. I see base communities more as an ecclesiological category than a sociological one: that is, I see them as more about Gospel than about class. I see the ecclesiology of base community as universally valid, though the particular form and shape of base communities will vary in every place where they are found. I see conflict between base communities and some members of the hierarchy at the present time as a regrettable and painful reality, but in no way whatsoever do I see rejection of the institutional Church as a part of what base community is about. And I see base communities as something fundamentally different from the many interest groups and pressure groups that are found in the first world. But more details of my understanding will emerge as the book unfolds.

Chapter 1 begins with some pictures and parables, because an image can clarify what we mean by base community in a way no number of words can. Chapter 2 continues to explain how I understand base community, by running through a series of questions that I have frequently heard asked in the first world.

Next I suggest three principal ways in which we can work towards base community in the first world. Firstly (chapter 3), we can work through other kinds of groups, which are not themselves base communities but which express much of the spirit and values of base community. Through these groups we can already begin to experience a new style of Church.

Secondly, there is the method of transforming a parish into basic ecclesial communities. Two examples come from the third world (chapter 4), two more from the first world (chapters 5 and 6). After presenting each case study I give a reflection on what it teaches us about base community.

Thirdly, we can begin right from first principles, among those who are not already practising Christians: I call this "starting from the street". Again two third-world examples (chapter 7) are followed by longer, more detailed accounts of two first-world communities, with a discussion of the points of principle raised by their practice (chapters 8 and 9).

Some diversity has been looked for in the choice of these four first-world case studies (Abbey Wood in London, Lakewood in Colorado, the Hope Community in Wolverhampton, and the Anfield Road Fellowship in Liverpool). Three are British, one comes from the USA. Three were initiated by men, one was started by women. Three are in working-class areas, one is amongst a middle-class community. Three are Catholic or originate from Catholics, one is in origin Protestant.

But before launching into chapter 1, with its pictures and parables, we need to get clear our terminology. What are we going to call these groups? Base communities? Basic Christian communities? Basic ecclesial communities? Or what?

A NOTE ON TERMINOLOGY

The area of the world best-known for basic Christian communities is Latin America, which is predominantly Spanish-speaking, though Brazil is Portuguese-speaking. "Basic Christian community" (or BCC) is the term most often used to translate the Spanish *comunidad eclesial de base* (or CEB, pronounced "seb"), or the Portuguese *comunidade eclesial de base* (also CEB, but pronounced "sebee").

It will be clear that a more literal translation of the Latin American term is "basic ecclesial community" (or BEC). Not only is this more accurate as a translation, but it is also theologically richer and more precise. The drawback is that this phrase is not yet very common in English usage, and many people do not understand what "ecclesial" means (it simply means "of the Church"). Avoiding the word "ecclesial", one can also speak of "basic church community", or "church base community".

But the CEBs of Latin America are also, if less frequently, known as *comunidades cristianas de base*. Almost everywhere it can be said that "basic ecclesial community" and "basic Christian community" can be used interchangeably.

This is not quite always the case, however. In the Philippines a distinction is common between "basic ecclesial communities" – which are more Church-controlled reflection groups – and "basic Christian communities" – which are more involved with socio-political questions and with community organization. In Italy there is also a distinction, where the *comunità ecclesiali di base* stand in clear contradistinction to the *comunità di base*, which are generally in conflict with the hierarchy. But my usage within this book will be to use "basic Christian community" and "basic ecclesial community" – BCC and BEC – interchangeably.

Another very common English term for the same entity is simply "base community". The context usually makes it clear that we are talking of a Christian community and not just, say, a local residents' association, with members of different religions or none. (Sometimes in Asia when people want to speak of a base community that is not specifically a Christian one they say "basic human community".) "Base community" is also a term I shall use in this book interchangeably with "basic Christian community" and "basic ecclesial community".

In Africa the prevalent term for the same kind of community is "small Christian community" (or SCC). This refers to exactly the same concept as BCC or BEC, even if the actual development in Africa is as yet a little more cautious.

Chapter 1

PICTURES AND PARABLES

Basic ecclesial communities make great use of symbol and imagery to make points. In this chapter I make use of some of their pictures – both verbal images and actual diagrams – to help explain how they understand themselves. The pictures all answer the question, "What is a basic ecclesial community?"

Cells

The basic ecclesial community is the basic cell of the Church. This was said at the great meeting of the Latin American bishops at Medellín in 1968: "The basic Christian community is the first and fundamental ecclesial nucleus . . . . It is the initial cell of the ecclesial structure."[1] Since then it has been repeated over and over again in all the theology of base community, and it holds the key to understanding everything. Everything I shall say will be in one way or another a spelling out of that claim. But what does it mean to say basic ecclesial community is the basic cell of the Church?

By "cell" we mean a cell as in a body. The body is made up of millions of living cells, reproducing and renewing themselves, and joined together to form the whole expanse of living flesh. So we are saying that the Church is a body, and that the smallest unit that goes to make up that body is a basic ecclesial community.

So this is the first and fundamental image: the cell of the body. Let us think about how cells work.

The cell is the very material of which the body is composed. The cell is alive and changing: old ones die and fall away, and new ones are born out of the division of existing cells, which grow large enough to reproduce. So too in the body of Christ the cells are

nucleus

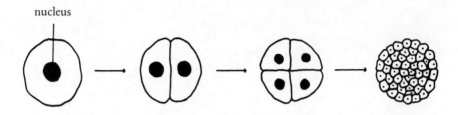

always changing. Base communities go out of existence and new ones come into being all the time. That is why it is always hard to obtain accurate, up-to-date information about their numbers and extent. Every time anyone tries to count them the figure is wrong even before they have finished counting.

Another point is that the cells of the body can only live by being part of the body. It would not be any use a cell thinking that because it formed its own complete circle it could exist by itself, drawing all its life-strength from its own self-sufficiency. Take it away from the body and it dies. You can keep it alive in a test-tube for a while, but not for long – it is an artificial existence.

So it is with a cell that tries to exist in isolation from the rest of the body of Christ. Even though each cell forms a circle, they are all dependent on each other, for it is only as a totality that you have a body, and it is the body which gives life to each individual cell.

Another point to make is this. A cell is centred around a nucleus – that black, mysterious mass in the middle that acts like a brain to the cell and controls its growth. What is the nucleus of the basic ecclesial community? Is it the priest? Of course not – that would be blasphemous. The community is centred around the mystery of God, around Jesus and the Spirit. "Where two or three are gathered in my name, there am I in the midst of them." (Matthew 18:20.) It is this divine presence at its midst that gives life to the base community, and that forms its focus, nourishment and inspiration.

Compare the picture of the biological cells with this diagram from a popular booklet[2] from the São Paulo diocese in Brazil.

The figure shows a single parish, already divided into six areas of basic ecclesial community, each with its own centre, represented by a tiny symbol of a meeting place or chapel. (The larger building shown is the parish church itself, which is the meeting place used

by the community living in its immediate locality.) The booklet is encouraging the formation of new reflection groups, shown as black dots, within each existing division. It is hoped that each one of these reflection groups will grow eventually to maturity as a full basic ecclesial community.[3] If the Church is to grow, a single cell must divide, and divide again.

Circles

The cell is not the only image for the base community that is circular. Many people have drawn diagrams of a base-community conception of Church, and the diagrams are nearly always based in one way or another on the circle. There are different ways of drawing the circle and its interrelation with other circles. But the fact that the circle is found over and over again, in different forms, shows that the circle captures something very important about base community.

The circle is often contrasted with another model – the pyramid or triangle. In the pyramid, we have a clear sense of who is above and in power and who is below and under control. In a Church conceived on the lines of a pyramid, hierarchy can become very much a dominating function, especially when it is assumed you must reach God through the apex of the triangle.[4]

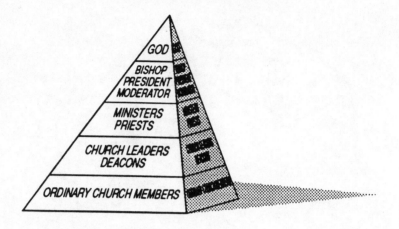

The base community structure, by contrast, stresses that the Holy Spirit is active within the circle of the people: initiatives can begin wherever two or three meet, rather than everything being handed down from the apex of the pyramid.

Here, for example, is how a catechetical booklet, used widely in Brazil, shows how the perception of Church has changed. From a rather static pyramid it has become a lively buzz of activity centred around the circle of faith.[5]

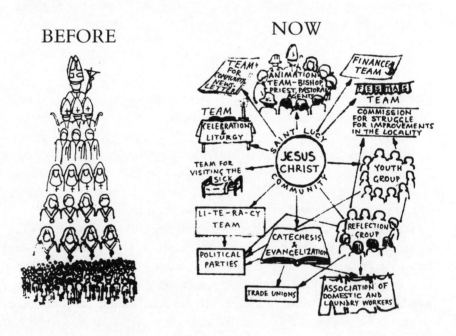

There is even a literal truth to the idea of the circle, for almost every base community meeting has people sitting in a circle. A circle emphasizes the equality of all present. No one is in front, and no one behind. Particular ministries are exercised from a common base-line. Everyone relates directly to everyone else, because from every point of the circle we can see all the circumference.

Interrelated circles

If we want to show the structure that links the different base communities, we do not have to use a pyramid shape, for we can also show it like this:[6]

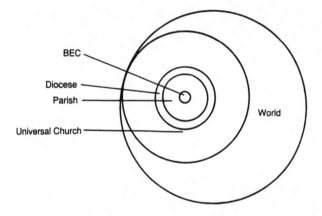

A similar diagram based on concentric circles is used by James O'Halloran,[7] whose work has been mostly in an African context and who therefore prefers the term "small Christian community".

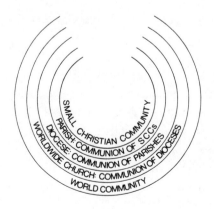

If we want to show how a number of base communities at the same level are related to each other (rather than just how a community is related to the other levels) we can make a circle out of the little circles, rather like a necklace, as in figure 1b below, used by Leonardo Boff. Here the presence of Christ is found at the heart of the circle, instead of being a distant influence mediated only through the chain of hierarchy above, as in figure 1a. (The pair of models are similar to the pair we saw on page 22.)

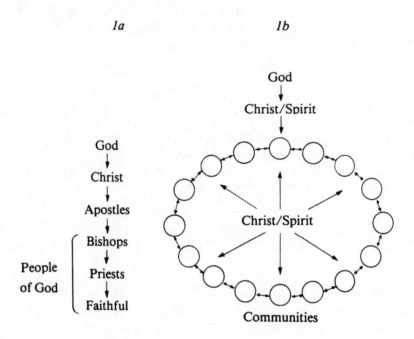

Figure 1, a and b. Conceptualizations of Church.

Boff gives his own explanation of what the two different models show. The linear model is of a conception of Church where "Christ transmits all power to the Twelve, who transmit it to their successors, the bishops and the Pope. The latter have been considered as the sole depositaries of all responsibility." But in the circular model the focus of God's power begins at the other end: "Before becoming visible through human mediations – those of bishop, priest, deacon, and so on – the risen Christ and the Spirit already possess a presence in the community . . . . In this understanding it is no longer difficult to grasp the ecclesiality of the basic Church communities, and to assign theological value to the various services which arise within the community as manifestations of the Spirit."[8]

A training booklet from the Lumko Institute in Africa[9] makes a similar point.

"It has pleased God to make men holy and save them not merely as individuals without any mutual bonds, but by making them into a single people." ↵↵

In the top picture people's primary mode of relating as Christians is between each other within a single small community: around the circle we see people visiting the sick, helping the needy, supporting the elderly, and getting inspiration from the book of the Bible. People relate to the central organization of the parish as an entire community, rather than as individuals. But in the lower picture, people only relate individually to the parish centre, with no interrelating between the laity. Obviously in the second model there will be many needs unmet because a single parish priest cannot attend to everyone, and there will be little experience of Church as community.

Every member of the small circle of the Christian community is also a member of the big circle of the parish, which we see here gathered around the altar for a common liturgy.

And each base community may also be represented by a delegate at the parish council, which then becomes another small, but second-level Christian community.

This is, of course, only one particular model of how the small com-

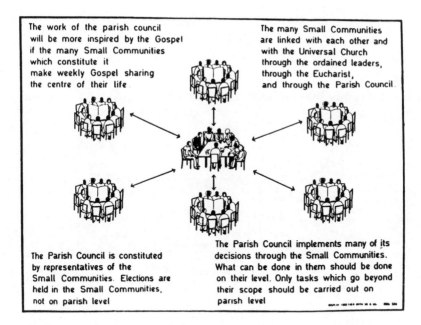

The work of the parish council will be more inspired by the Gospel if the many Small Communities which constitute it make weekly Gospel sharing the centre of their life

The many Small Communities are linked with each other and with the Universal Church through the ordained leaders, through the Eucharist, and through the Parish Council

The Parish Council is constituted by representatives of the Small Communities. Elections are held in the Small Communities, not on parish level

The Parish Council implements many of its decisions through the Small Communities. What can be done in them should be done on their level. Only tasks which go beyond their scope should be carried out on parish level

munities could work. Not every base community will be a part of a parish that has a parish council. Nor will every parish with small communities meet regularly together for common worship (in some parts of the Amazon region, for example, it can be several days' journey from one end of the parish to the other). Nor has every base community achieved open lines of communication with its parish centre: in some places the parish clergy are still suspicious of base communities, so that the rare groups that do manage to get going have to struggle for recognition. Specific models for the relationship of parish to base community therefore vary, but the underlying point remains the same: base communities relate to each other, whether through the parish or through another network, and they form an ever-widening network of circles.

Circles can also be used to map out the difference between base communities and interest groups, associations or movements. Most parishes in the first-world Church have a number of small groups operating, such as prayer groups, rosary groups, justice and peace groups, Journey in Faith groups, and so on. There will also be local branches of particular movements or associations like the Neo-catechumenate, Communion and Liberation, the Legion of Mary, St Vincent de Paul Society, Christian Life Communities, and many others. There may also be short-term groupings formed for specific ends, like ecumenical Lent groups, groups to organize the bazaar, groups who are making a parish retreat, and so on.

Parishes structured in the old way, with several movements and interest groups but without base communities, find that the same

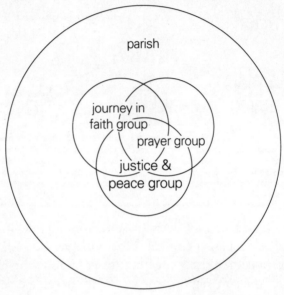

people tend to be involved in all the activities. And so the different groups overlap each other, forming a common core of activists, while the great majority of people do not belong to anything.

This is largely due to an innate rule of group dynamics: for efficiency a small, dedicated nucleus naturally tends to form, which actually gets things done. The same rule applies in base communities. There is still usually a small, dedicated nucleus; but instead of this being eight or ten people in a group of, say, a thousand, it is four or five people in every group of, say, fifty. You will never get a comparable number from the wider parish group to become active unless a proliferation of smaller groups requires their involvement, and at the same time provides a safe environment for them to lose their shyness and find out their capabilities.

Here is the way the Lumko booklet perceives the difference between the old parish groups and base communities. We see in the picture on the left how individuals are drawn from all over the parish territory to membership of associations (represented by flags), but the great majority remain isolated, uninvolved individuals. In the picture on the right, however, everyone is gathered into their local community, whether or not they belong to an association as well. Everyone is involved somewhere.

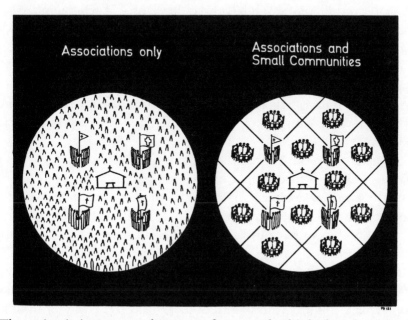

The point is important, because often people think that the way to respond to the problems of an inactive parish is to start a new movement there – something that has been found to inspire a lot of people in other places, like the Neocatechumenate, or the Charismatic Renewal. And indeed these kinds of groups can help many people. But we can see from diagrams like these that they can only provide a partial answer. Some people will become members of these groups, but not everyone will, because that style of spirituality or that particular interest will not appeal to all.

If we want to reach all the parishioners then we need the kind of community that is not an optional extra for the keen, but is the very way in which one is inserted into the Church. On this conception, you do not join the Church first, and afterwards consider joining a basic ecclesial community as well. Rather, to join the Church is to join a basic ecclesial community, and to join a basic ecclesial community is to join the Church. The base community meeting becomes the primary, basic meeting, while parish activity happens at the second level. You might go to the parish centre when you organize with a bigger group to have a bigger celebration, or when you make use of office facilities (typewriters, copying machines, parish registers, flip-charts) that are shared for the whole area.

Traditionally the absolutely basic level of Church membership *was* parish membership. But parishes are not real communities, for although everyone knows the priest, few people know each other. That is why base communities were started, as a breaking down of the Church into smaller units than parishes,[10] to form real communities – communities where people can turn and face each other, and where they can know and love each other, and where everyone can be known and loved.

Clearly, then, the basic ecclesial community does not replace the parish entirely. We can see the base community as the stepping stone into the parish, just as the parish is the stepping stone into the diocese, and the diocese is the stepping stone into the universal Church.

The Lumko booklet makes these points effectively with the model of beads strung together, such as could be used as a teaching aid for a sermon. The idea comes across very simply and very clearly, and if some may be concerned that it makes too neat and institutional a model, it is important to point out that this is not a way of making base communities serve the parish, but, of making the parish serve base communities. The whole sermon is reproduced on pp. 31-3.

Solar system

The solar system is another variant on the theme of circles, and for this model I am grateful to José Marins and his workshops.

The first circle here is the core of the old-style parish – the priest, the sacristan, the organist, perhaps a parish sister, and possibly one or two others who are always at the centre of things. This group is like the sun, in that all parish activity circles around them, under their control and influenced by their attraction.

In orbit around the sun are the planets. These might include one or two catechists, the person who runs the bingo, the man who runs the bar, the lady who types the newsletter, the servers, the church cleaners, the helpers at the fête, and so on. The sun provides instructions for this second group, and they in turn provide problems to be

As several beads form one necklace, we form communities

Last week our Parish Council took an important decision, after long consultation with all members of our parish. You remember that it decided to invite all members of our parish to form Small Christian Communities. The poster depicting the life of such Small Christian Communities is still displayed here on the side-wall of our Church. But still, many of us are wondering what all this will mean for us. We know that it is not just the idea of a few people but it is actually Christ's call to us. It is something which already the very first christian communities did, and it is described wonderfully in the bible. But still, we may find it an unfamiliar idea. Let me try in this sermon to make it a bit clearer. Allow me to use something visible, some beads, to illustrate this idea of Small Christian Communities.

Let me compare the many members of a congregation to the many small beads I have in this glass dish.

Each one of them feels attached to the parish Church. This here is a small cardboard picture of the parish Church. The members of the congregation go to the Church for the services, and when they need the advice or the help of the priest who stays at the Church.

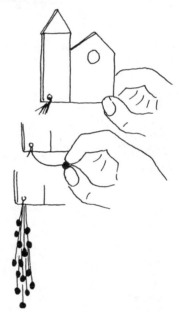

It is as if each one of these beads would like to be connected to the parish Church. Here is one bead tied to the Church by a little string. (*Show one of the beads tied to the picture of the Church*).

The others, too, would like to be connected to the Church. (*Show the whole bunch of beads, tied to the cardboard Church, some shorter and others at a longer distance*).

Each one is concerned about his own connection to the Church and to the priest. He or she knows, of course, that there are many others who also belong to the same Church, but it does not concern him or her too much. If I move one of these beads (*take one only*), the others remain undisturbed and unmoved. It does not concern them what this one bead does.

But this was only one possible way of belonging to the Church. Here is a different one (*take the second dish with beads and the cardboard picture of the Church still lying flat*).

Again we speak of a good number of christians who belong to a congregation. They, too, have a parish Church. *(Show only the cardboard picture, not yet the beads which are attached to it).*

The christians of this congregation also want to belong to the Church, but in a different way. They do not wish to remain separate individuals in the Church. They realize that to be a christian means that we are not attached separately, just as individuals, to the Church or to the bishop. They are aware that we belong together. They want to be interconnected. This is what they did: *(show 8 or more beads tied together in a circle).*

They formed a group. It is a small group, since only in a small group can people know each other. They form a small community of christians who want to belong together, to pray together, to help each other and to serve others.

This small community was formed of people who lived next to each other. This is why we can speak of a neighbourhood community. They meet once a week to meditate on God's Word. At these meetings they also decide what they can do for others.

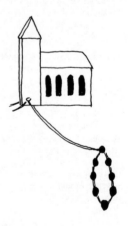

This does not mean that they want to separate themselves from the rest of the congregation. They do not want to be a Church of their own, without connection with the whole Church. This Small Christian Community is connected with the whole congregation. *(Show also the string which ties the small circle to the picture of the Church.)*

Not only the one small group of christians of this congregation wants to live as a community, but many others have the same wish. They, too, formed such Small Christian Communities. Here is another one. *(Show another ring of beads tied together and to the Church).* One parish could have ten, twenty or even more such Small Christian Communities. In each of them the christians feel they belong together, but they also realize that they belong to a whole congregation. They know that they are members of the universal Church.

If I take one single bead *(try to hold one of the beads tied together),* I can hardly do so without moving the others. This was easy with the first congregation, where the movement of one individual did not affect the others at all.

The christians of the Small Communities know that this can cause some difficulties. To pray together and to work together can mean that we have to make some sacrifices. But these difficulties and sacrifices help us to grow together. They make us a community. They help us to realise that we are one people, we are the Church.

A large congregation of several hundred or of several thousand christians cannot live as one single community. Searching together in the scriptures is only possible in a smaller group, so that each one has a chance to say what he or she feels. Personal relationships are only possible in smaller communities. They would not be as small as the 8 beads, but they might consist of 30 or more people in each community.

Dear brethren, this is what is meant by the decision of our parish to form Small Christian Communities. We feel that it is Christ's call to create closer ties between us, to overcome our individualistic attitudes. This will not be easy, since we have become accustomed to pray, to work, and to live as individual christians only. We will have to show much understanding for each other during this initial stage of forming Small Communities. Let us help together so that we may become Christ's Church in a more genuine way.

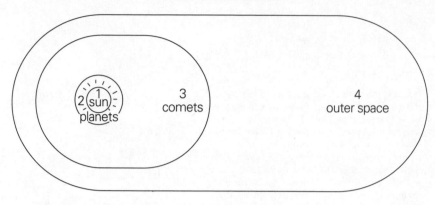

sorted out by the sun. Everyone is kept very busy, sun relating to planets and planets relating to sun. The parish agenda makes for a full life.

At a slightly further distance is the area through which comets pass. The comets are people who come and go in the parish. They might come once a week. Or they might come once or twice a year, at Christmas and Easter. Or they might come once or twice a lifetime: at baptism, marriage and funerals – their own, or those of their family or friends. But they do not really interact with the parish centre. They are faces that appear briefly, and then disappear again. The majority of baptized Christians are in this group. Year by year their participation in the Church becomes more and more occasional, until they lapse from Christian practice altogether.

There is a fourth area, outside the solar system. Here you find people with no relationship at all to the Church. This is the largest group: at least 70 per cent of humanity is here. This is a group to which the traditional solar system simply does not relate. However, Jesus' mission is to take the Gospel "to the ends of the earth", in other words to go out into this area. In most parts of the world, if there is any interaction between the first two groups and group four, the idea is that people from outer space should come into group three, and then hopefully progress into groups one and two.

The vision of basic ecclesial communities is that the movement should go in the other direction – not that outsiders should come closer to the sun, but that committed Christians should go out into space. And that they should go there, not to bring people back into the inner orbit, but rather to build Christian community out there. This is done by converting group three from occasional comets into a network of basic ecclesial communities. Then there will be not just one sun around which everything is in orbit, but a number of different centres, each providing strength for its members, and situated all over the place.

From each base community, Christians go out in mission to those who have no contact with the Church. In area four they will work with others who are engaged in the sort of work that Jesus promoted – it might be race-relations work, or trade unions, or health, or education. A work area like this in area four can be called a "missionary base".

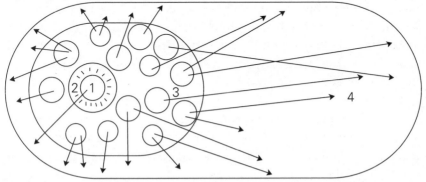

In missionary bases, Christians do not have to work only with other Christians. Indeed, it is often a bad thing to be separatist about this work, as though to devalue the efforts of those not working under a specifically Christian label. But Christians working there will need specifically Christian support for their work, and for understanding the spiritual and theological implications of the challenges they meet. This Christian support will come from their ecclesial base – the basic Christian community. In this way of looking at the relationship of Church to world, we see much better what mission – or sending out – means.

Pastoral cycle

The pastoral cycle is yet another circle. But this circle is a diagram of something rather different – not the structure of the base community, but its way of operating.

What does a base community do? What happens at its meetings? What kind of work does it undertake? How much is action and how much prayer? These are questions often asked, and there is no recipe that can be given in reply.

Rather, we need to understand more deeply what the Church is for. How should the Church be spending its time, and how should it be relating the needs of prayer and activity? If we understand that, we will have the answer to what the basic ecclesial community should be doing.

Earlier this century a widespread movement known as Catholic Action popularized a way of operating known as "See-Judge-Act". A Belgian priest called Joseph Cardijn was much involved in getting these groups going, in movements like Young Catholic Workers and Young Catholic Students, which helped laity to live out their vocation in the world with some serious thought and commitment. Catholic Action groups would follow the See-Judge-Act cycle, as the basis for their meetings.

The idea was to help people notice what was happening in their own environments – whether as workers, as students, as young people, as intellectuals, or wherever they were: this was the "See" part. Then they tried to assess the situation according to Christian principles, with the help of scripture, Church teaching, theological exchange, or anything else that would assist a Christian perspective: this was "Judge". Finally they planned what they should do in those situations: this was "Act".

Over a period of time, of course, the progression became cyclic, as their "Act" led to a new situation for them to "See" and "Judge". The cycle was found to be very effective, as it helped Christians to be practical, so that their meetings were not just a "talking shop".

When the basic Christian communities began in Latin America in the late fifties and sixties, they drew quite consciously on the method they had learnt from Catholic Action: See-Judge-Act. And they began to add another two steps after "Act" – "Evaluate" and "Celebrate". This balance of elements has been an important insight in their way of being Church. For example, a document signed by fifteen Mexican bishops said that, "The same method of the BECs (to observe, to think, to act, to celebrate, to evaluate) speaks to us of a renewal in our hearing and communicating of the Gospel."[11]

Evaluation is an important part of judging our own actions, as

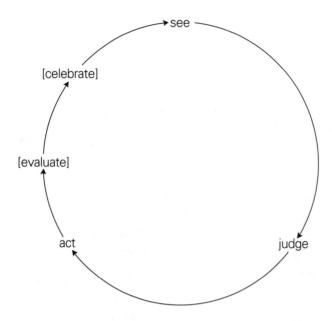

part of the planning for future actions. It is not just a matter of saying that an action was successful or unsuccessful, as though to give it a mark. It is rather to ask questions like, "What was the most successful part? What were the unforeseen problems? Can we make any improvements for next time?" In other words, evaluation always looks to the future, not just to the past.

Celebration is important, because without it life is so serious and intense that it becomes dull and loses the touch of enjoyment that is such an essential stimulus to carrying on. We can celebrate by finishing a meeting with a drink in the pub or a coffee in the local bar. And as Christians we also celebrate in liturgy – eucharistic or not. If our liturgical celebrations do not relate to our lives and actions, then they become very barren and fail to nourish us. Our times of worship should be real celebrations, not just in name but also in spirit. They should spring out of our lives and struggles, and feed us for the work that is ahead. They are moments of memory, consolidation, strengthening, thanksgiving, and enjoyment.

Most parishes in most parts of the world spend so much time on church services, and so little on action, that our view of what the Church is for becomes very unbalanced, and we can really begin to move away from the teaching of Jesus, with his strong emphasis on action. We can tend to think that being a practising Christian is a matter of saying a lot of prayers and going to church often, rather than of living in the way he taught us to live. We can forget the words of Isaiah, when he said that we do not even worship God by such devotions unless they are combined with the exercise of social justice.

> Bringing offerings is futile;
>> incense is an abomination to me . . .
> even though you make many prayers, I will not listen;
>> your hands are full of blood.
> Wash yourselves; make yourselves clean;
>> remove the evil of your doings from before my eyes;
> cease to do evil,
>> learn to do good;
> seek justice,
>> rescue the oppressed;
> defend the orphan,
>> plead for the widow.
>
> Isaiah 1: 13, 15–17; NRSV

Again, most parish liturgies do not spring out of the life of the local community, but go on as though in a sort of capsule of their own. It is all laid down word for word in a book that comes from overseas, and there is usually no attempt to interpret that celebration in terms of the culture and environment of the local people. But if we understand "Celebrate" as the last item in a cycle, rather than as something standing in isolation, then we transform our whole approach to worship.

Sometimes the ideas of See-Judge-Act-Evaluate-Celebrate are phrased in a different way. One such way, that has become very popular, is known as the pastoral cycle (or circle). It is also sometimes known as the circle of praxis. One of the presentations of it that has influenced many people comes from *Social Analysis: Linking Faith and Justice*, by Joe Holland and Peter Henriot,[12] where it is presented as shown opposite.

CAFOD[13] uses the pastoral cycle, or the See-Judge-Act method, as a way of running meetings for their campaign groups (see p. 40). The cycle is no sort of rigid programme, that has to be followed

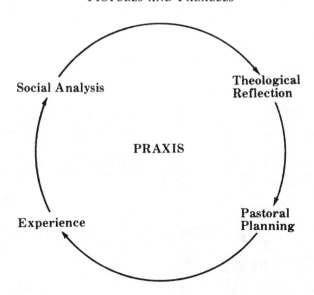

in order. Rather, these are all elements of the Christian life, that should all be found in some form. Otherwise the Christian community will become unbalanced, and untrue to the Gospel.

It is often said that the whole point of basic Christian community is that faith and life should come together. It does not matter if a group begins with scriptural reflection, and goes on to action (as when a prayer group becomes a base community – some CEBs have begun like this), or if a group begins with action, and goes on to prayer (as when a campaign group becomes a base community – other CEBs have begun this way, too) so long as the cycle from-faith-to-life-back-to-faith is present in one way or another. Both starting points are equally valid.

The tree

An image for base communities that has been used over and over, in varying ways, and with great creative potential, is that of the tree. Often it is a spoken or written parable, rather than a visual diagram, but both may be found.

Every time we hear a phrase like "from the roots up" (as in the book *The Church from the Roots* by José Marins and team) this image is evoked. Here is a typical use of the tree image, made by Clodovis Boff:

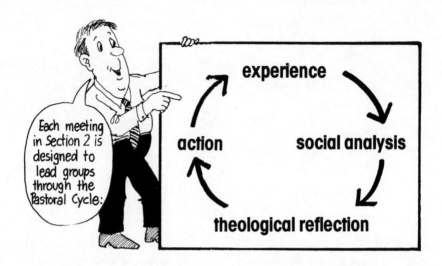

Meetings start with a learning experience and groups are encouraged to analyse what they have learnt and identify causes. They are then led to judge the experience from a basis/understanding of their faith and relevant scriptural texts are provided. This may lead them to take action which in turn leads to more experience and so the cycle continues. Basically the meetings follow the pattern:

How, anyway, can the fabric of the Church be renewed except from below, starting with the ecclesial cells constituted by small communities? It seems to me an illusion to think that the Church can be revitalized from the top and through mere institutional reorganization. Of course, these institutions need to join the dance, but it won't be they which will start it off. The life of a tree comes from the roots and not from the crown![14]

The great Brazilian biblical theologian, Carlos Mesters, who has worked so tirelessly with base communities, is fond of developing the tree imagery in one way or another.

Our communities are like a tree. In the ground, invisible to the eyes, are the roots, whose tips are at once the strong and the weak point of the tree. They are its strong point because through these thousands and thousands of tips the tree sucks up the sap of the earth. They are its weak point because the ends of the roots are fragile, so fragile. The least shock damages them, bruises them. Without this permanent fragility in the roots, however, the tree cannot rise up out of the ground healthy and strong, cannot replenish itself and keep on living. This fragility must be maintained, even cultivated, certainly not eliminated! The higher the tree, the deeper and broader the root must be. This is what gives the tree its strength.[15]

Liberation theologians have clearly thought a great deal about what we can learn from the growth of a tree, and in this they are of course following the example of Jesus, who uses the tree as a favourite theme in his parables (Matthew 13:31–2; Luke 6:43–4; John 15:4–5).

An exercise based on the tree is used in a number of workshops to help people answer for themselves the question, "Who am I?", and then share their answer with others. No genuine community can form unless each person is welcomed and known as a unique individual. Then, out of the sharing of individual identities, a group identity can grow. The tree is used to help people think of the roots of past, family and culture that formed them, the trunk of present concerns that sustains them, and the flowers and beginnings of fruits that are their future.[16]

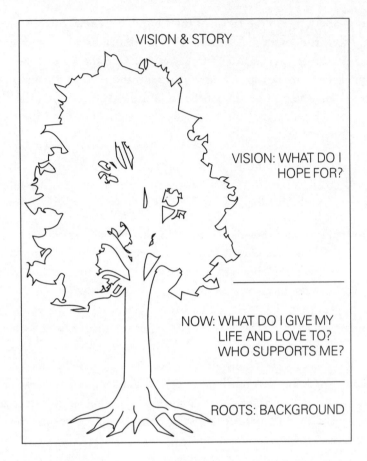

As people share who they are with others through an exercise like this, a small, strong community of trust is formed. Properly understood there is no conflict between the cherishing of the individual and the cherishing of the community, for the individual both springs out of community, and is nourished by it. It is only when individual values are taken alone and get out of relationship with the interests of the community that we find "individualism", so often criticized as a sin by the base communities.

The symbol of the tree is developed in many ways. But just as there is a literal truth to the circle image – because base communities sit in circles – so too there is even sometimes a literal truth to the tree image: when a community in a hot country has no building to meet in it often meets underneath a tree. An African Textbook, *Training for Transformation*[17], uses a tree as a logo which appears at the heading of every chapter,

and the cover shows a small group sitting underneath the same tree.

I will end this section on the tree symbol with Leonardo Boff's vivid image from *Church, Charism and Power*: "Church", he says, "is an event that may take place beneath a mango tree."[18]

> The group may meet under a huge tree and every week they are found there, reading the sacred texts, sharing their commentaries, praying, talking of life, and making decisions about common projects. It is an event, and the Church of Jesus and the Holy Spirit takes shape under that tree.[19]

The river

Another image that comes up again and again is the river. The story is told of how a tiny trickle begins, perhaps formed by a few drops of rain running off a leaf: this is the beginning of a basic Christian community, as one by one, a few people get together with a common aim. But it is not the only trickle. Soon it is noticed that other little rivulets are forming too, and running into each other. As they join, a more definite stream can be discerned. In the same way, once the people begin to organize, little beginnings can be found here and there all over the place. Each one taken alone seems so weak and small, and yet something has been started which keeps on growing.

Stream joins stream, and soon we have a river, making its steady way through the plains, and growing broader all the time. In the same way, base communities network together and become a powerful force together. By now there is no stopping the river. Even if a dam is built, it can only hold back the waters for a while, but as they build up they will overflow the barrier. And so base communities can meet many discouragements and persecutions, including setbacks from their own Church institution. But as long as more water is running into the river from sources far away, there can be no stopping the power of what has been started. The river will plough on relentlessly to the open sea, which is the vision that lies ahead.

This story is often told. Opposite is a well-known version from "The Journey of a People" slide programme used in São Paulo in 1980:[20]

The story is recalled also in the final Letter from the Sixth Interecclesial Assembly of Basic Ecclesial Communities held at Trinidade, Brazil, 21–25 July 1986:

> The struggles of the people are like the springs of water that bubble up from the ground and become a stream that flows down the mountain until it becomes a river. And the river, with God's strength and the unity of the people, will grow until it sweeps away the old society built on the exploitation of the people.
>
> The popular movement has many streams: the trade union, the political party, the residents' association, the various movements – of the landless, slum-dwellers, marginalized women, fisherfolk, leprosy patients, disabled children, women, blacks, and indigenous peoples. Some of these are great rivers, others still small streams. But the struggles told by the people show that they are growing throughout Brazil, and from resistance struggles they are turning into struggles of conquest. It is the political project of the people which will channel the water of these streams into the great river which will do away with a society based on profit and oppression and found a society of the kind that God wants. (10–11)

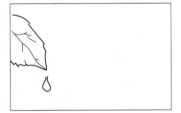

73. In spite of all this, our movement exists. It started slowly,

74. like morning dew which, drop by drop, makes a small thread of water.

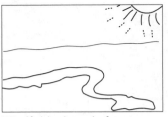

75. If this thread of water does not meet any other, it will dry up and disappear.

76. But if, little by little, it does meet other ones,

77. it slowly becomes a stream,

78. then a larger and larger river,

79. a river flowing to the sea of our hopes.

Pulling the Church down to earth

There is one final image that evokes dramatically what basic ecclesial community is about, and that is the Church pulled down from the clouds to earth. Here is a statement by the Communities of Santa Catarina in Brazil that paints a verbal picture:

> The old Church was a fortress. It began from the top down, guided by the hierarchical system. The people were kept on the fringes. The people had neither voice nor place. The Pope, the bishops and the

UM JEITO NOVO DE SER IGREJA

9

O QUE ESTAMOS VENDO NO DESENHO?

priests were considered to be the owners of the Word and ministries. The Church built for itself a place in the clouds, far from reality, unaware of the suffering, anguish and hopes of the People of God . . . . The Church was pulled down. The transformation happened when the people felt the need to have a Church journeying side by side with them . . . . Base communities sprang up. People gathered in "human-size" groups to reflect, unite and move into action. The Word and ministry have been given back to the people.[21]

This image is represented pictorially in one of the Brazilian booklets we have already looked at,[22] as the illustration for their ninth and last session, which is titled "A New Way of Being Church" (see opposite page).

An almost identical picture is found in *Training for Transformation*,[23] except that the people are African, not Latin American, and that their building has not reached the heights of grandeur of the Brazilian cathedral.

The accompanying text here says: "The hierarchical old institution with 'princes and palaces' is evolving into the Church of the people, and the Church of the poor." But there is hardly a need to explain the meaning of pulling the building down from the clouds to where the people are, on the ground beneath. The picture says it all.

A British equivalent of this idea is found in a document from the Anglican diocese of Leicester,[24] which shows a woman deacon pinning down the balloon of the Church to the ground, in case it floats away from reality.

A slightly different European version of the relationship between people and institution comes from a survey produced by Ian Fraser, called *Wind and Fire*, illustrating an interview recorded in Naples in 1984 with Ciro Castaldo, co-ordinator of the Technical Secretariat of Italian Base Communities. This cartoon, which is by Ray Price,[25] illustrates the more anti-institutional approach of some European groups called by the same name of "base communities", especially in Italy, Spain and Holland, where the ecclesiology (that is, theology of the Church) has some differences from that found in the third-world base communities.

Attempts are being made to recover us for the institution . . .

Again we see a group of people on one side, and a building with a spire on the other. Again, a rope links them, and the rope is pulled to bring the two groups closer together. But whereas in the Brazilian and African pictures it is the people who are trying to pull the institution towards them, in the European illustration it is the opposite: the institution wants closer links, but the people resist.

In the third-world examples, it is the people who recognize that the institution belongs to them, as though to say, "Let us work together to bring our Church down to us, to share in our reality." In this European example, on the other hand, the community members do not feel themselves a part of that Church: they seem to say, "Let us not get sucked up into the institution. Let us stay here, at a safe distance, where we can keep our autonomy."

This interpretation becomes clearer in the text of the accompanying interview with Ciro Castaldo:

> We do not "want recognition from the institution". . . . . What is really happening is that attempts are made to recover us for the institution . . . . What we want to do is to undermine the nature of the institution and its theology. Faith, in history, must not be pinned down dogmatically.

Another expression of this more anti-institutional kind of European approach is found in a document from the Secretariat for the Basisbeweging (that is, Base Movement) in Holland, which says that base communities "operate on the fringe of or outside the churches". And in "reaction to the Roman Catholic hierarchical models and the reformed synodal model", the base communities have "a divergent view of questions concerning office and eucharist".[26]

This difference of approach has been remarked upon by some Latin American theologians. Dominique Barbé, for example, writes in *Grace and Power* that the Latin American base communities "are strongly connected with the bishop; whereas in Europe the base communities, often having a different social origin and being communes rather than communities, are mistrusted by the hierarchy, and vice versa" (p. 89). Marcello Azevedo too, in *Basic Ecclesial Communities in Brazil*, says that "basic communities that have arisen in Europe (particularly France and Italy) and the United States since the 1960s seem to be quite different in nature and thrust when compared to those of Latin America" (p. 8). They have "a connotation alien to the ecclesial character of BECs in Brazil" (p. 20). In the "communities outside Latin America, one is immediately struck by the note of dissent vis-à-vis the hierarchical Church. In Brazil these communities see themselves as ecclesial and call themselves such, clearly stressing their respect for the hierarchy, their attachment to it, and the active role of bishops, priests and religious in their establishment and development. This point is frequently brought out by those who write on BECs, just as it is consciously noted by the populace and by pastoral agents. In Europe and North America ecclesiality is not denied or rejected. But it is seen as a rediscovery of community that often sets itself in opposition to the hierarchical Church, which is regarded as noncommunitarian and an obstacle to the growth of community." (p. 68.) Reservations have also been expressed to me verbally by other liberation theologians and Latin American pastoral agents.

I therefore have some hesitations over identifying the European groups called "base communities" as our local, inculturated version of the Latin American communities. There are many similarities – similarities for example in commitment to the marginalized, in lay involvement and in liturgical creativity – but at the same time there are differences in the way they relate to the rest of the Church. Between seeing the base community as the basic cell of the Church, and seeing the base community as on the fringe of, or outside, the Churches, there seems to be a major theological divergence that can in no way be accounted for by cultural differences between the first world and the third world.

Third-world basic ecclesial communities show no signs of breaking off from the institution. This is all the more marked for the difficulties and injustices they have often endured for the sake of remaining in communion with their hierarchy. The base communities of the third world could never say, "We do not want recognition from the institution." The people love their bishops, and when the bishops treat them with misunderstanding and rebuffs, they are deeply hurt; they grieve and struggle to convert their pastors, feeling themselves inseparably linked to them, as branches of the same tree, as water of the same river, as cells of the same body. This difference is not unconnected to the fact that members of European "base communities" are nearly always middle-class, while members of third-world base communities are nearly always from the lower classes. But it goes deeper: the difference is theological as well as sociological.

For these reasons I have decided it would be too complicated to include within the scope of this book the European groups that explicitly call themselves "base communities". My exploration of first-world examples will not depend on whether a group calls itself a "base community" or not – in fact most of my case studies do not use that term – but rather on whether it seems under analysis to belong to the same ecclesiological family.

That is also partly why I often opt for the term "basic ecclesial community": it is a term which is not used in the European "base community" development,[27] and so helps to avoid confusion. At the same time it acts as a constant reminder of our starting point and fundamental principle: a basic ecclesial community is the basic cell of the Church.

Chapter 2

SOME FIRST-WORLD QUESTIONS

This chapter will take many of the most common questions I have heard from people in the first world, as they grope towards discovering what a basic Christian community is in its essence, and what it might mean in the context of the developed world.

I should stress that even among people with a lot of experience of base communities there is some diversity in the way the term is used, and a consequent diversity in the answers they would give to these questions. But here are the direct replies I would give, based upon my understanding of basic ecclesial community as more of a theological than a sociological category.

1. Can you have a first-world base community?

Yes. Some people think that basic Christian communities belong to a different culture from ours – the culture of the third world – so that they would not be appropriate for first-world society; but that is to assume that third-world culture is all of a piece. In fact the communities have been formed successfully in a huge range of cultures.

It is generally agreed that the first basic Christian community was not, strictly speaking, somewhere in Brazil sometime in the sixties, but was the community of Jesus and the Twelve. And following on from that, the early Church communities were all basic Christian communities. Once it is recognized that basic Christian communities go back to the New Testament, we can see at once that they cannot only be for Latin America (with maybe the Philippines and parts of Africa thrown in as well). They must be for everyone, for all cultures, all times, and all places. There could not be a form of Church that the third-world and the early Church shared in to the exclusion of the other nations.

It is often said that base community is a new way of being Church. But if it is also an old way, that goes back to the beginnings, then in a sense there has always been basic ecclesial community, for as long as there has been Church. And so, wherever the Church is found, basic ecclesial community is found too, in a sense. And yet, in another sense, basic ecclesial community is always in the making, just as the Church is always in the making. Not every part of the Church has really found out what it means to be Church. In fact very few have. Some parts of the third world lead the way on this, and those are the ones that we generally recognize as having achieved the status of basic ecclesial community.

We should use the term selectively, but not too selectively, or it becomes an impossible ideal. When we want to talk of the ideal we should talk of the Reign (or the Kingdom). Basic ecclesial community is a provisional, inadequate structure – but the best we currently have – for working towards the Reign of God, just as Church is a provisional, inadequate structure for working towards the Reign. Church and base community are structures for the journey, not for the final destination.

There are many stirrings and experiments in the first world, but we cannot yet say that first-world basic ecclesial communities have clearly emerged – certainly not in a coherent form or in a widespread way. Though basic Christian communities are for the first world, we are only beginning to explore what that means. The communities lie in store for us, like a great future peeping out from under the covers.

And so we live in an age of reverse mission. In earlier centuries Europe took the faith to the ends of the earth. In our own day it is Europe who must relearn the expression of the faith from the countries she once colonized. We live in an age where the United States is a major political power, for good or ill, on the world scene; but in religious terms she must humbly learn from those countries over which she has exerted political dominance.

2. Can you have a middle-class base community?

Yes, no one is excluded from the Church, no matter what their class. In the same way, no one is excluded from the basic Christian community – neither because they are middle-class, nor because they are working-class. In a middle-class locality, it would be normal to have a middle-class base community.

However, two qualifications need to be made. One is that the basic Christian community has a particularly strong awareness of the option for the poor as an intrinsic element in Gospel commitment. So a middle-class base community, or a middle-class member of a base community, would be called to make an option for the poor. This does not mean stripping oneself of one's class member-ship and pretending to be a different type of person. But it does mean relating to one's class in a new way, and living in the spirit of the Magnificat in which the mighty are humbled and the humble exalted.

The second qualification is that we do not often find basic Chris-tian communities yet among the middle classes, just as we do not often find them yet in any clear or widespread way in the first world. All the Church is called to the vision of basic Christian community; but it is the poor of the third world who have responded first and led the way.

There are many reasons adduced for the middle-class slowness in forming base community. Some say the middle classes are too individualistic, so they have no urge to do things together as a com-munity. Some say the middle classes are too self-concerned and do not want to make an option for the poor. Some say the middle classes are so weighed down by their money and their success that they have no desire for transformation, and their eyes are not open like the eyes of the poor to recognize the freshness of the Gospel message. And so on.

On the other hand, probably most of the readers of this book are middle-class, which is at least some indication of an interest in community, option for the poor and the freshness of the Gospel message. In fact, it is middle-class Christians in the first world who have heard about the base communities and are interested in doing something about it, though – aware of the option for the poor – their first efforts will not be among the members of their own class but among the poor.

It may be expected that the middle classes, like the first world, will get there in the end.

3. Can you have a base community which is not based on the neighbourhood?

Yes, sometimes people come together more naturally and effectively on another basis, such as for work or according to country of origin. Just as there are industrial chaplaincies, student chaplaincies, chaplaincies for foreign nationals, and so on, so equally there can be basic Christian communities along similar lines. Those from minority groups are often able to express their culture better when they have a chaplaincy, or a base community, for themselves (and recognition of culture is very important in a base community).

However, the most common basis for a basic Christian community is the locality. A geographical basis enables the community to be more inclusive and less of a clique; for a basic Christian community is more than a group of friends, more than an interest group, more than a protest group. Unless there is some recognizably open criterion for membership – such as anyone who is a student in a particular college, or an employee in a particular industry, or a national of a particular country – then a community which is not related to the locality is at risk of losing its "base" and ceasing to be a basic cell of the Church.

Of course it is a marvellous thing when a group of friends get together to pray, read the Bible, and to put their faith into action together. And normally such groups are extremely welcoming to new members. But though we would readily call that a Christian community, we would not normally call it a basic Christian community, because it usually does not present itself as a basic cell of the Church, but rather as an extra group, complementary to basic Church membership.

If we think of how the Church can divide up its mission throughout the world, so that every person has somewhere to turn, then we are likely to end up by carving up the map – first into dioceses, then into parishes, then into local communities. That way every place is covered, and through every place, every person is covered too. Any other basis runs the risk of forgetting someone who does not easily fit into other groups. The Church must forget nobody. When the neighbourhood is taken as the basis then children, for example, are seen as full members, rather than just being relatives of adults who are members.

Of course the geographical divisions must not be arbitrary, or they will cut through natural groupings and stifle the Spirit. They will become, in short, like the national boundaries imposed by colonial powers on third-world countries, which sometimes cut right through natural tribal groupings and left problems for future generations. In some parishes, because of their size, different groups are sometimes lumped together that are unlikely to jell as a community – a working-class housing estate with a middle-class area for example, or two different styles of working-class community, as in the Abbey Wood parish we will look at in chapter 5. It is precisely in cases like this that a geographical sub-division can enable more natural communities to form and to flourish.

4. Can you have a residential base community?

Sometimes basic Christian communities are initiated by a small residential community (for example, two or three sisters, maybe with a few laity as co-workers) who come to live in an area to work among the people. However, this small community of pastoral agents would not normally be called the base community: the base community would be the Christian community that begins to form among the indigenous people of the neighbourhood, probably helped by the resident community's influence and inspiration.

A residential community is a different kind of Christian community, because its membership depends on something more than the basic qualification of being a Christian – it is for people who are able to make the commitment of actually moving in and living together. However, the residential community will probably fulfil many of the functions of basic Christian Community for its members: for example, it will be in the residential community that they find most of the Christian support and fellowship they need. But if we want to discover how to form, or how to join, a basic Christian community, we would not be expected to pack up and move house into a commune!

5. Can you have a base community which meets once a month, or less?

It is a long and firm tradition, not only in Christianity and in Judaism, but in other religious traditions too, that once a week is a good rhythm for community worship. When a community wants to meet much less than that, it may be because the community is a secondary commitment over and above the basic Christian unit, which is probably the parish.

6. Can you have a base community of four or five members?

Yes, some basic Christian communities have begun as small as this, or have been through bad periods when their numbers were so reduced. However, it would not be a healthy sign if the community did not grow larger. It is difficult to operate as a basic cell of the Church when you are this small – it is more like a part of a cell, than a complete cell such as we would call the local church.

There are two basic rules on size. On the one hand, the base community has a missionary, evangelizing dimension, helping the faith to spread, and so we would expect the community to grow. On the other hand, if the community becomes so big that the members can no longer know everyone at a personal level – maybe just know their names, and maybe not even that – then it is natural for the group to subdivide, either to form two or more separate communities or to have additional meetings as sub-groups. If some sort of sub-division does not take place then we are back to the vices of the old parish system, where people can walk in and out of church and never say hello to anyone or have any genuine experience of community.

As an extremely approximate guide, people seem to find that anything between fifteen and fifty regular members is a feasible size for a basic Christian community. But at any single meeting, there might be present half that number, or fewer.

7. Can you have a base community which is not Christian?

Yes, but it won't be a basic *Christian* community. The Sri Lankan theologian, Aloysius de Pieris, speaks of basic *human* communities because in his country, where Christians are very much a minority, it makes sense to form inter-faith communities rather than Christian communities.

In South Africa, the networks of street groups struggling on behalf of the black population have had many features in common with basic Christian communities, except that they have not been specifically Christian, even if all the members were in fact Christians. In that context, the racial struggle overrides all else in importance.

The same could apply in some first-world contexts. For example, in an area of Britain with a high Muslim population, people might justifiably decide to put their efforts into forming a local community that included the poor, Muslim population and that was not a Christian community. The interests of justice might be better served by forming such a group, than by trying to establish a basic Christian community.

None the less, since there is always a need for Christians to meet and worship, even when their principal struggles must be made in solidarity with non-Christians, there will always be a place for a basic Christian community – that is, for a moment in which the Christian members of a struggle meet together as Christians, even if it is only occasionally.

8. Can you have an ecumenical base community?
Yes, but it is not as easy a question as many people think. This is probably the number one question with regard to first-world basic Christian communities, and it is an extremely difficult one. I will look at the problems first, and later at the points in favour.

As we have seen, a basic ecclesial community is the basic cell of the Church, and that means it does not exist in isolation, but is part of the body of Christ. Catholics cash this in terms of the basic ecclesial community being in communion with the parish priest, in communion with the bishop, and in communion with the Pope. Protestants make whatever modifications are required by their different ecclesiologies.

Once a community becomes ecumenical, that network does not exist in the same way. Now this obviously has attractions for the members of a base community, in that it gives them greater freedom. No one can order them to do anything, or stop them doing anything, because there is no body which has authority over them.

But the flip-side of this advantage is that no authority also implies no communion. There is no structure holding the community in communion with other communities. Of course there are all sorts of informal ways in which we meet and exchange and share with other Christian groups, but here we are talking more about who we know and who we feel we have something in common with. Communion, however, depends on something more objective – on a structural unity.

Problems can arise from the looser, more informal networks. For example, it can occasionally happen that, after we get to know a group better, we find they have ideas or practices we are not comfortable with – perhaps they do not believe in the divinity of Christ, or perhaps they believe women should be subordinate, or perhaps they levy a tithe to support their own organization – so we are not so sure we belong together after all.

But in the full communion that is implied by Church unity, we are in communion with those we have never seen or spoken to, with those perhaps who we do not like, with those whose language we do not speak, with those of the past and the future and not just of the present. We do not have to find them out and size them up and decide if we belong together or not. All that work has already been done for us by the organizational structure.

Where there is not communion, there are consequent difficulties over the eucharist. Catholics are not allowed to take part in eucharists celebrated by ministers of other denominations, and although many Catholics break this rule, it remains an individual decision: some will partake and others will not. There is no such thing as a eucharist that includes everybody. And where the community cannot share the same eucharist, it clearly lacks an important element of Church: it is more of a Christian group than a basic cell of the Church.

This is related to another disadvantage – that an interdenominational community is usually an extra group for the keen, so that among the parishioners of different churches a few especially committed ones will meet together as an ecumenical group in addition to going to their own church. An extra group for the keen is not the *basic* Christian community, and it does little for the ordinary Christian. Generally, ecumenical groups are middle-class endeavours, because they operate among those who are informed enough to have an opinion about what you can do together, and what you cannot; what the Church ought to be working towards and what we can do about it. And so ecumenical groups are not always the best way of exercising an option for the poor.

On the other hand, when trying to form basic Christian community among those who are not already churchgoers, the opposite tends to happen. Evangelization is very difficult if there is any sense that different denominations are competing for members, and an ecumenical community is often then the most apt way of exercising an option for the poor. As the liberation theologian, Carlos Mesters, has said, "The most ecumenical thing we have is life itself." In other words, whenever we are truly trying to link faith to life, we are impelled in an ecumenical direction.

Another point in favour of ecumenical communities is this. Many people feel strongly that no new Christian enterprise of any sort should be started that is not set right from the beginning on an ecumenical basis. Otherwise one is simply perpetuating the divisions of the past, by continuing them in the new structures.

Furthermore, there is little point in Catholics setting too much store on the universality of the Catholic Church, when so many Christians are not Catholic. A truly universal Church – a catholic Church with a small "c" – must include more than Roman Catholics. And so we have to admit that, in this sense, a Catholic base community lacks full catholicity, and because of this, it lacks an element of the fullness of Church. From this point of view, there is a sense in which an ecumenical community can be more fully a basic cell of the (future, really universal) Church than a merely denominational community can.

In short, we have to admit that both denominational and ecumenical base communities are lacking something in what it means to be Church, though they lack it in different ways. We need to think through carefully the consequences of any path we take before we get too far along it. At the same time we do not want to be frozen into indecision by the dilemma.

The way through is, in principle, clear enough: what we can do together, we do together; and what we cannot do together, we do apart. That principle might work out in practice something like this. The different churches of a district would meet to plan their pastoral strategy of base communities together. They would map out the ground, and agree on common geographical boundaries. Then within each base-community area there would be the possibility for Christians to meet together, either as smaller communities of the respective churches, or as a larger ecumenical community.

At times, for example when celebrating the eucharist, or when responding to a communication from the diocese, it would be appropriate for members of separate churches to meet separately, and so continue to express their membership of a wider Church than just the local community. At other times, for example when planning Christmas carol-singing, or when constructing a rota to help in a neighbourhood centre, or when reading and discussing the scriptures, it would be appropriate to meet as an ecumenical group, all together, and so build towards the united Church we are all looking forward to.

In practice, of course, particular communities would find out for themselves the balance of meetings that worked best for them. But there would be no structural impediment to closer ecumenical ties forming year by year. Nor would there be any structural impediment to the particular denominations – at a diocesan or national or even international level – fully owning their local community as a basic cell of their Church.

More reflections on ecumenical communities will be found in the sections on the Hope Community and the Anfield Road Fellowship – both ecumenical communities, but of different types.

9. Can you have a base community that does not celebrate the eucharist?

Yes, but it will lack something in its expression of being Church. It will not experience being a basic cell of the Church in the full sense of the word unless the members are able to celebrate the eucharist together at least occasionally. How occasionally does not matter enormously: it is more important to discover what it means to be a eucharistic community than to have frequent celebrations of the eucharist.

This leads on to a further question. Can you have the eucharist in a basic Christian community without a priest? Because the eucharist is part of the fullness of Church, and because a base community wants to be recognized as a basic cell of the Church, some communities in the first world have taken on themselves the authority to celebrate the eucharist. In this way the members are demonstrating that they regard the community as Church, whether or not the other churches accept it as such.

However, it is an important part of the theology of base community developed from third-world Catholic communities that the base community cannot operate in isolation from the rest of the body. Since the eucharist is an act not only of the community physically present, but of the universal Church (one bread, one body), the small community cannot validly celebrate a eucharist that the rest of the body fails to recognize.

10. Can you have a base community which does not read and discuss the Bible regularly?

No. The Bible is so basic to Christianity that it cannot be ignored. Of course we can read the Bible at home by ourselves, but one of the great insights of basic Christian community is that when the Bible is read and prayed about and discussed in community it yields insights for the community, and not just for the individual. The liberation theologians point out that the Bible is the book of the people of God, and so the on-going people of God, that is, the basic Christian community, should read and celebrate it as *their* own book.

The only proviso that needs to be made is that it is not a matter of making a book into an idol, but rather of treating it as a synthesis of the revelation of Jesus. Otherwise the illiterate, who cannot read the Bible, become second-class Christians (in some third-world communities all the members are illiterate). Moreover, in the Middle Ages few people had Bibles other than monks. Biblical stories and teachings can be remembered, retold and reflected on, not just read out of the book.

11. Can you have a base community which does not have a group social project?

Third-world base communities have come to be so connected with group projects like food co-operatives, or sewing classes, or literacy schemes, or building ventures, that people from the first world might feel they would not have a basic Christian community unless it too shared some kind of a group social project.

Such a project might be a good idea, but it might also happen that the members of a community were involved in diverse projects, not organized by specifically Christian groups. Then the Christian community meeting is the chance to bring the bits of their various lives together, and find mutual support in their different commitments.

What is essential is to recognize and implement the Christian call to make an option for the poor. Then that option can be expressed in whatever way is appropriate – in a group social project, in a number of social projects with non-Christian groups, in members exercising their professions among the poor or for the benefit of the poor, in subscriptions to associations working for justice, and so on.

Many of the kinds of activity undertaken by third-world base communities are more suitably the responsibility of the State in first-world countries. A base community may need to decide whether its energies would be better employed in campaigning, for example, for a hostel for the homeless rather than in trying to provide one from their own resources.

So there is no one model for the way a base community should put its faith into action. All that matters is that the link-up of faith and life should be very much on the agenda of the community, and that the way of implementing it is discerned in the light of the local situation.

12. Can you have a base community which is initiated or organized by the institution?

Some people have taken so seriously the idea that a base community operates from the bottom up and not the top down, that they are unwilling to allow any influence to come down from the top. But that is to go from one extreme to another.

In practice, the great majority of basic Christian communities in the third world have been initiated by priests or sisters or seminarians, and the greater the encouragement from the institution and the local bishop, the more the communities have flourished. There is no contradiction here, because the pastoral agent acts as leaven in the dough – which is the people. The whole point is to activate the laity, but that activation generally happens when there has been a spark from someone who is probably in the institution, though not "institutional" in style.

More than that, most third-world basic ecclesial communities have needed the on-going presence and encouragement of some sort of pastoral agent from the institution – not to organize what they can do for themselves, but to keep up the encouragement and provide expertise when asked for.

And so there is no need to shun the initiatives of the clergy or the parish in the first world either. The institution can certainly take an initiative on the formation of a base community, though whether it succeeds will depend on the people from the base. But the direction of the work must be constantly towards facilitating, enabling and liberating the laity into taking on the maximum responsibility and ministry that they are capable of.

13. Can you have a base community where the local priest is not supportive?

Yes. The Church is the people, and the community finds its ecclesial validity through the nucleus at the centre of the cell, through Jesus found in the midst of the people. Unfortunately it is by no means uncommon that the parish priest is suspicious or even hostile of local base communities. Sometimes these communities receive support from other priests, perhaps from religious congregations rather than from the diocese, and this enables them to have the eucharist, but they might also have to struggle on alone.

In the first world, where there is not yet an established network of base communities, it could well happen that a community would form before the parish priest was ready to understand and support what was going on. Or he might try to interfere and to decide on matters that the community should decide for themselves. This is painful for all concerned, and it can often lead to a watering-down of the base community idea, or alternatively it can result in confrontational attitudes.

It takes a long time to change the expectations of clergy roles that have been operating for centuries. But there is absolutely no need for any group to ask permission of the clergy before meeting, praying, and acting as a Christian community, so long as they do not take on sacramental roles that need the authority of the wider Church and not just of the small community alone.

14. Can a whole parish be a base community?

The more we look at what it means to say a basic ecclesial community is the basic cell of the Church, the more aware we become that from some points of view the nearest thing that we have in the first world is the parish itself.

One of the big differences between the Church in the first world and in the third world is the size of parish. Many third-world parishes stretch over huge areas, and include ten times as many parishioners as in the first world. Many people can never reach the parish church at all because of the distance and the lack of transport, and that is why the Brazilian base communities began in the sixties – to provide for the Christian people in the absence of the priest.

If we want to build basic Christian community in the first world, then, can we look to converting the parish itself? Of course it is not a matter of taking a parish and calling it a base community, but of altering the whole way in which the parish functions, so that the same group of people are transformed from the base upwards.

Much will depend on size. There are many Anglican parishes in rural England, for example, where the regular congregation is only a handful. Certainly in these instances it would make sense to try to inspire both vicar and people to operate in a new way, understanding the Church as the people, not the building and the clergy. It would be quite wrong to leave aside these existing local Christians, as though they were some irredeemable fuddy-duddies, and try to start something new with a different lot of people. The whole point of a base community is its potential for transforming people: it does not depend on choosing the "right" people for the community.

But the majority of first-world parishes are still too large for everyone to know each other. (Our very rough rule of thumb for a genuine community was somewhere between fifteen and fifty regular members.) A first-world parish would then need to find a logical way of subdividing into two, five, ten, or twenty areas, in order to find the right size of unit for the most effective work. But it may be very difficult to communicate a new way of being Church when people have so many existing assumptions about the way a parish operates.

15. Can you have a base community which is a group within the parish?

If in most cases the whole parish is too large to be a basic Christian community, then can a few people within a parish start up a group to be a basic Christian community within the parish? Yes, they can, but they must be careful on what basis the group is founded.

The chances are that a few people from all over the area, who are "into that sort of thing" – into justice and peace and liberation theology and so on – will form a group among themselves. The "basic Christian community" will then be a group of like-minded people, and there will be little chance of the dynamic spreading to the rest of the parish. The "basic Christian community" will come to refer to a certain sort of person, interested in certain sorts of activity, and will lose its universal quality and its potential for transforming the entire Church.

The same comments would apply if the base community drew its membership from a number of different parishes, or from a number of different denominations, except in those cases it would have even less leverage to affect the style of the ordinary Christian.

On the other hand, if a basic Christian community was started as a group within the parish, which started, not from a scattered group of friends sharing a common outlook, but from a more objective base, then the outlook might be different. Most obviously, it could start in one geographical area of the parish, with all parish members of that locality invited, so that locality then acted as a pilot group for what might be done elsewhere. Or it could start with all those who regularly attended a particular mass on Sunday. Or it could start as a group for – say – Caribbeans, or Hispanics, where there was an obvious objective basis so that everyone within those categories was included.

Needless to say, it is far more likely that a pilot group will spawn other basic Christian communities within the parish if the priest is supporting and publicizing what is going on, and encouraging other groups to start. More will be said on these topics in the chapters on "Starting from the Parish".

16. Can you have a base community where the members do not go to church?

Yes. There is no reason why a basic Christian community could not start among a group of people who were so alienated from the existing church options that they did not go to church at all. One of the great insights of the basic Christian communities is that the Church is the people, not the building or the clergy.

In practice, however, it is not so simple. Why is it, given the wonder of the gospels and the inadequacy of the existing Church institutions, that little groups of non-church-goers all over the place are not meeting together, reading the Bible, and starting something new that is closer to the original Christian vision? In practice we find that those chafing at the bit to re-create what Church should really be about, are usually themselves church-goers, even if frustrated ones. Indeed a remarkable proportion of them are themselves ordained ministers.

The Christian life is, as Jesus said, like a seed that takes time to grow, needs soil and water and sun and so on. It does not just pop up without a nurturing environment. And whatever the inadequacies of the existing Church institutions, they have managed to nurture many fine plants.

We could put it this way: you need at least an experience of a bad Christian community before you can have the vision of a better Christian community.

We are more likely to see a basic Christian community growing among non-churchgoers when a pastoral agent or agents comes to work among the people, introducing them over a period of time to the invitation of the gospels, along the lines of some of the examples in the chapters on "Starting from the Street".

17. Can you have a base community which has no contacts with the local churches?

No. Even if a basic Christian community did begin among people who were not church-goers, it is inconceivable that they would not want at some stage to establish contact with other local Christians, unless they really were a sect – that is a group that keeps itself separate and thinks of itself as the only authentic Christian body.

A community that spends too much time on its own often ends

up developing a rather idiosyncratic version of Christianity, with particular practices or doctrines of its own. We need to keep in regular touch with each other to grow as an organic whole, as a single vine, as cells of one body.

For this reason, large congresses and assemblies have been an important and joyful part of base-community life, when there is potential to celebrate on a bigger scale than a single community ever could.

Even those who do missionary work at a distance from the institution feel themselves very much in contact with it. This applies whether they are literally miles away from any church, stuck in the jungle somewhere, or whether they are living rather at a psychological distance – perhaps on a run-down housing estate from which no one ventures out to the more middle-class areas to "go to church". It is not important that either these missionary agents, or those they work with, should be trotting back for church services all the time. But it is important that all parties know that missionary work is what the whole Church institution exists for in the first place, and that there is a lifeline of support and resources for those who are reaching out to where the Church has not yet penetrated. Only then can it be understood that the further away from the established structures the missionary agent is working, the closer he or she is to the very heart of the Church.

Chapter 3

FINDING THE SPIRIT AND VALUES OF BASE COMMUNITY IN OTHER KINDS OF GROUPS

In the attempt to implement basic Christian community in the first world, I would like to suggest there are three possible lines we can follow, each good, but distinct from each other. Which we choose will depend on our situation and possibilities, and on the way each of us is called to work for the Gospel.

One way is to start from the parish, and to make a conscious attempt to convert the parish into a community of communities. This is a very fruitful approach, but it is really only practicable if we happen to be the person responsible for parish policy – the priest, or at least a member of a parish team where the vision of base community is shared.

Another way is to start right from first principles – "from the street". Then we would gradually come to know, and share the Gospel with, the people of a neighbourhood – preferably, but not necessarily, a poor neighbourhood. This is a very radical approach, and it does take a long time.

But the method that this chapter focuses on is to start from the kind of groups that already exist and already have something of a base-community spirit. There are all sorts of little groups and initiatives where a lively, forward-looking, option-for-the-poor way of approaching the Gospel can be found – justice and peace groups, third-world groups, prayer groups, interest groups, ecumenical groups, movements and networks and conferences of many kinds. Once we begin to come across people with this kind of involvement, we find how many excellent things are going on in the Church that belie its dull, conventional, conservative reputation.

These initiatives already exist in the first world, and already they are signs of hope. They are, as Clodovis Boff says, "like the first tiny bubbles which appear at points on the surface of a pan when it is about to boil. The heat isn't yet sufficient to set all the water moving – as seems to be happening in Latin America at the moment – but the pinpricks which herald this situation are multiplying right across the surface of the European Church."[1] In ways like this, we can join our efforts to something good and vibrant that is already going on. As more and more people are touched by the influence, so more and more of the Church will absorb the spirit of this new life.

There is only one point that needs stressing. Most of the groups I am speaking of are not in themselves basic Christian communities. Nor, in most cases, will they ever be basic Christian communities. Their function is different.

They may be interest groups, for those from a wide area who share a common interest. They may be action groups, for those who already express other aspects of their spiritual life in other contexts. They may be protest groups, or ginger groups, for those who are campaigning on a particular issue or set of issues. We may be talking of a one-off meeting at a conference, when people share an intense experience together during a few days, and then disperse. None of these groupings are designed to be basic cells of the Church, and we should not attempt to force them into that pattern.

There may of course be ways in which such groups can be enriched by the insights of base communities. They might be helped, for example, by exploring those stages of the pastoral cycle that they are weakest in. They might be enhanced by the use of symbol, or by a more serious attempt at organization. Some few might even be able to develop fruitfully into base communities, though this is not to be regarded as a norm.

We should not for a moment think that if a group is not going to become a base community then there is something wrong with it or that it is a waste of our energies. The aim is not to convert everything in sight into a base community, but to help each group develop to the full according to its own function. Building basic ecclesial communities, properly so called, is an important task, but it is not the only task that faces the Church: working for justice is more fundamental and has many other avenues.

The situation is complicated by the fact that some people in the first world use the term "base community" more loosely than I have defined it in this book, so that some such justice groups or interest groups have been called "base communities". For example, many residential communities and many Christian feminist groups have been called "base communities".

In fact, my first example in this chapter is of a Christian feminist liturgy. But I would hesitate to call such a women's get-together a base community as such, though it shares the spirit and values of base communities. As an interest group of like-minded people, of one sex only, drawn from a wide area, concentrating on one primary issue, it lacks something of the inclusivity and universality one would look for in a basic cell of the Church. Moreover in this particular example, the women met in a conference situation rather than as a regular group.

And yet by participating in groups such as this we are already working towards the future, in which the spirit and values of a new way of being Church may penetrate to both sexes, all classes, every age-group, and every culture. We may need Christian women's groups, but we also need a Church in which everyone – women and men, middle-class and working-class, adults and children – can share their life and zest.

A women's Holy Week liturgy

In spring 1990, an ecumenical group of women gathered in a conference centre to celebrate Holy Week together. Here are two accounts of the same event, told by participants:

> I am writing a week after the return from Harborne, having spent the intervening days trying to pass on to others something of the significance of the women's Holy Week for those who took part. But how difficult it has been! How to communicate the intensity and variety of the experience? The layered richness of the liturgies, the constant surprises as we discovered new levels in ourselves and others, the renewed colour and shine of the Easter themes as we viewed them through a different prism?
>
> The core of the week's activities – the raw material from which we made our spiritual discoveries – was ourselves. And what a varied lot we were as we gathered together that Tuesday evening after supper,

viewing each other with some anxieties, if little suspicion. During the course of the week we were between twenty-four and twenty-eight in number from different generations, backgrounds, experiences and levels of belief, yet, thanks to the superb organization and the activities planned for us, we rapidly got to know each other at a level which astonished us all. Each day we sat in groups looking together in an open but carefully structured framework at our experiences, thoughts and feelings in the light of the Easter themes. Each session ended in liturgical celebrations which invited participation but never demanded it. And we learnt from each other. Listening to everyone's contributions in humility and expectancy, we received spiritual sustenance: women ministering to each other in love and faith, bringing Christ powerfully alive.

Now, a week later, the images still crowd my mind: the beautiful higgledy-piggledy web we wove as we struggled to articulate our views on community; the warm silkiness of the Maundy Thursday water on my feet; the stunned silence as we sat in semi-darkness after an anointing ceremony, absorbing the spiritual shock-waves; the weight of the stone that we passed round our circle to symbolize suffering, and the bread that took its place after the sharing of our burdens; the results of our determination to be honest with each other – the two young women whose creed began, "We believe, by the skin of our teeth . . .", and my own efforts not to rap out "Jesus is Lord" when asked to give a testimony. Above all I remember the repetition and interpenetration of the circle symbol: the spherical candle which centred our activities all week (not, as Philippa pointed out, the usual shape for a candle), the circles we sat in, the round stones we stared at on Good Friday, the candles and eggs we passed round in our Easter liturgy, the image of planet Earth (very much in our minds all week) – all of them pointing towards an image of wholeness we were striving to envision.

We weren't serious all the time, of course. A plentiful supply of tea, coffee, wine and fruit juice made the kitchen a natural focus for socializing, and we sat there in ever-changing groups, mainlining Rich Tea biscuits and talking endlessly. The party which followed our Saturday liturgy (the resurrection came early for us this year) was joyous and lively, and continued until 1.30 a.m. with Brid leading us in singing song after song. Our repertoire wore a bit thin towards the end – we hit "Puff the Magic Dragon" about 12.30, and selections from *The Sound of Music* at about 1.00. (Have you ever *listened* to the words of some of those songs??) Lala's suggestion of "Goodnight Irene" brought the evening to a suitably maudlin close.

An Anglican from the fundamentalist/evangelical tradition, I was initially apprehensive both about my welcome, and my ability to participate in strange, exotic rituals. "I'll die," I thought, "if I have to do anything too toe-curling." But I was spared terminal embarrassment, and treated always with warmth, acceptance and love. Back home, charged with a renewed mission, I have planted my seed, both literally and metaphorically, joined CWN,[2] and bought a knitting pattern, needles and wool. And my ideas about nuns have undergone certain changes too . . . .[3]

A second woman recalls the same events:

Women, strangers and friends, getting to know each other. Sharing in small groups, allowing space and building trust.

We each choose a flower and place it in a vase in the centre of the large group. The final display represents our beauty in diversity.

A role-play on the woman anointing Jesus' feet. Our group had no Jesus – "I'm coming," called Alexina from the other side of the room. Anointing each other with scented oil – "It is a beautiful thing you have done for me" – and it was.

Weaving a web of different coloured ribbons – weaving in our joys and sorrows, weaknesses and strengths. New symbols draw forth new meanings and everyone contributes.

The web is spread out on the floor when we gather for Holy Thursday liturgy. So it is with many of the week's ideas and symbols which are gathered in and built upon to form a rich cohesive whole . . .

Friday – and the liturgy begins first thing in the morning in the garden. If we see the earth as a symbol of God's body, then God is damaged through our destruction of the earth. We remember the earth as mother and gather handfuls of earth to bring inside and place in a small rock garden in the centre of the room.

There is much sorrow shared in our small groups. Some suffering seems inexplicable – maybe all we can do for those who suffer such pain is to be with them as the women were with Christ at the foot of the cross.

Back in the main room and the largest of the rocks is lifted from the earth and passed round. We feel how heavy and unyielding it is.

Saturday is a day of waiting and we begin our liturgy in darkness, waiting at the tomb. Then Mary Magdalene meets Christ and is charged with a mission – I have a Gospel to proclaim. Stirring music, and the open Bible on the floor is lifted up and, held high, carried slowly round the dimly lit circle. Then it is held out to each woman in turn – we all have a Gospel to proclaim.

Each woman makes a statement of belief, lighting her candle from her neighbour's as she does so. As we proclaim our faith in a Christ who chose Mary Magdalene as the first witness of the resurrection and a God who is revealed in the faces and voices of women, the room gradually fills with light.

We share wine and tiny chocolate Easter eggs. The eggs are a symbol of new life and wholeness – and they're fun.

We finish with Carly Simon's "Let the River Run". Scarves have been gathered and knotted together and we hold these above our heads, swaying in time to the music.

Then a heartfelt hug for everyone and the party begins. Several times during the evening the basket of eggs is picked up and passed round again. There is no division between the sacred and the secular, between our worship of God and the rest of our lives.

Women celebrate death and new life. We celebrate our strength as women, our affirmation of ourselves and of each other, the empowerment that comes from devising our own liturgies and choosing our own symbols and discovering that they make God real for us. We celebrate the joy of the risen Christ.[4]

Reflection

In these vivid and imaginative accounts there are many themes that strike common chords with the base communities that are found in the third world.

First of all we cannot fail to be impressed by the liturgical creativity, with a fertile use of symbols, old and new: "New symbols draw forth new meanings and everyone contributes."

In particular, the "repetition and interpenetration" of the circle symbol is striking. Right from the beginning of this book we have seen how the circle is a key image of the base community. Here we find it in the spherical candle, the circles people sat in, the round stones and eggs, and in planet earth itself.

There is a rediscovery of new meaning in old traditions, as people write their own creeds. And there is a focus on the scriptures, while the custom of holding the Bible triumphantly aloft is similar to Brazilian practice.

Then we can see something of the Church's universality represented in the variety of ages and backgrounds, which spanned fundamentalist/evangelical to traditional Catholic. Even though they were all women, probably all middle-class, and all motivated to go away to a conference centre for a new way of celebrating Holy Week, there is still an expression of "beauty in diversity".

We notice the way sharing and trust can build up through a community small enough for everyone to get to know each other. They share "in small groups, allowing space and building trust". Even in the space of a few days, people become awakened through this nurturing environment to an awareness of new potential: "we discovered new levels in ourselves and others".

There is "an affirmation of ourselves and of each other", a "ministering to each other", and an "empowerment". And out of empowerment comes a spur to new proclamation of the Gospel, as they return home "with a renewed mission".

Then there is that characteristic union of faith and life: "There is no division between the sacred and the secular, between our worship of God and the rest of our lives."

Last but not least we can draw attention to the importance of relaxed socializing – what Latin Americans would call *alegría* – as the women gather in the kitchen "in ever-changing groups". And celebration of faith overflows into celebration of secular culture, with the fun of a late-night sing-song.

Overall we can say that a Christian women's group of this kind can provide one of the best ways currently available in the first world today of experiencing the life and freshness of a base-community kind of Church. For the reasons I have already given, I prefer to say that such groups have many points in common with base communities, or that they are a way of working towards base communities, rather than that they are base communities themselves. But we must recognize a diversity of usage here, for the term "base community" is used increasingly in this context.

The Congress of Black Catholics

There are different kinds of groups that suffer discrimination, in the Church and in society. We turn now to the marginalization of the black community. The following account is abbreviated from a much longer report I wrote, with the collaboration of Betty Luckham, about Britain's first Congress of Black Catholics.

Almost 200 black Catholics gathered at Digby Stuart College, Roehampton, over the sweltering weekend of 13–15 July 1990, for the first-ever Congress of Black Catholics to be held in this country. The participants were British Catholics from Asia, Africa and the Caribbean.

The Congress met in a mood of what Haynes Baptiste from Dominica, the Chairperson of the Congress Steering Committee, described in his opening words as "love, joy, hope, rejoicing, and celebration". And if anyone had had the slightest doubt about commitment to the one, united Catholic Church, Anthony Lobo from Goa, chairperson of CARJ,[5] would have put their minds immediately at rest: "We remain committed to unity – one Lord, one world and one Church." After the greetings, Cardinal Basil Hume delivered the opening address. After the Cardinal, the Apostolic Pro-Nuncio, Luigi Barbarito, spoke.

After warm applause and appreciation for their presence and support, came the keynote address by Leela Ramdeen, Vice-Chairperson of the Cardinal's Continuing Committee for the Caribbean Community. From the first paragraph of Leela's speech, the atmosphere became electric, as she put her finger on the way the delegates felt. "We have uttered our cries of pain and frustration for years," she said. "We are here because we are not apocalyptic Christians. That is, we are not a sit-down-until-judgment-day-and-do-nothing people of God." There were cries of "yes, yes" around the room, and she supported her cry for action with some words of Paul VI: "It is not enough to recall principles, state intentions, point to crying injustices and utter prophetic denunciations," the Pope wrote. "These words will lack real weight unless they are accompanied . . . by effective action."

Leela said, "We are here: both black and white as God's rainbow people." And she asked, "How do we touch the rainbow? How do we touch the Christ that is in each of us?" A sense of worth is crucial. "We need to affirm each other a lot more – to instil pride in our culture, background, heritage and faith in our ability to achieve." Also precious is a commitment to the unity of the Church. "The dogged determination that many black people have to remain within the Church is a testimony to their faith." And she quoted a vivid statement by a Caribbean Methodist woman who stood strong in her Church membership despite remaining "invisible" to many white Christians: "I'm like a tree God planted. I'm in and I'm not coming out."

The evening finished in a spirit of togetherness and with an act of worship – a lively singing of an Alleluia, and of two choruses: "God forgive my sins in Jesus' name" and "Nothing can separate us from the love of God". Then the tired, but hopeful and greatly stimulated delegates found their way to the bar, and thence to bed.

Saturday began with a morning act of worship, at which the story of Cornelius' conversion was read. Heard in this gathering, the application to our own day was startlingly obvious. Peter's comment that "God shows no partiality, but in every nation anyone who fears him and does what is right is acceptable to him" (Acts 10:34–5) is as relevant today to black and white people, as it was then to Gentile and Jew, and there was a reverent mood of shared understanding in the chapel.

After breakfast everyone met in the lecture hall for three talks. The first speaker was Beverley Prevatt Goldstein, a social worker born in Jamaica. Beverley took as a theme for her talk, "Survival – We Are Here". "We are not victims, we are survivors" was an important insight, and she read this extract from *And still I rise* by Maya Angelou:

> Out of the huts of history's shame
> I rise
> Up from a past that's rooted in pain
> I rise . . .
> Bringing the gifts that my ancestors gave

I am the dreams and the hope of the slave
I rise
I rise
I rise

Though some may have learnt negative things in the struggle we have "a great deal to contribute to the Church in terms of spirituality and community."

The second address was by Revd Braz Menezes from Goa, who is the first black ordained deacon in the country. Braz brought some biblical input, asking, "How did Jesus deal with ethnic minorities?" He reflected on the story of the Samaritan woman at the well, and referring to the woman's question, "How is it that you, a Jew, ask a drink of me, a woman of Samaria?", he asked pointedly, "Who are our Jews and who are our Samaritans today?" Jesus leads the woman from distinctions to an openness to all humanity.

"When we look at two-thirds of the world today we rejoice that the Churches are growing there among the poor, so it is no longer Gospel *to* the poor, but also Gospel *from* the poor. And the new insights and perspectives of the Gospel are coming to the whole Church from the community of the poor." It is a matter of "mutual giving, receiving and hearing".

The third speaker, Bishop Patrick Kalilombe (originally from Malawi and currently director of the Centre for Black and White Christian Partnership at Selly Oak Colleges) delivered a powerful, amusing and inspiring speech. He said that "black" meant "on the margin, on the underside of history". "I may not like it," he said, "but I am on that side. I have seen during the ten years I have been in this country," he explained, "that bishop or no bishop I belong to the black community." This experience was reinforced every time he went through British Customs, where he was always stopped. Someone suggested that if he dressed as a bishop he would have no problem, so one day coming from Belgium he went through in his full pontificals. "That day they really stopped me." For an hour they searched him. "For once, they said, this must be a real crook."

His final message was that black people "have been too long silent". Up till now the whites "have been the ones doing the talking for us" but the time had come to change that. "They have been very good.

But they cannot talk for us . . . . At some stage there is a word which only you can say, and that word has to come out." Bishop Patrick, like Leela the night before, was greeted with a standing ovation.

Saturday afternoon was devoted to workshops, which provided a forum for many personal stories of hurt to be shared. In some workshops a lot of anger was released. In others, there was a lot of pain (one leader had to say at one point, "What we are talking about is very painful: that is racism. If you want to cry, cry"). Others progressed in a more gentle manner.

Views on how to deal with the problems were not always the same. Some individuals and groups called for more black vocations to the priesthood and more black participation of the laity. But others explained that they were not happy to be a token black person: they would not, for example, agree to read at mass or to take up the offertory gifts, as though all were well, until some of the underlying issues of racism were looked at.

At the end of the workshops the participants returned to the lecture hall for a short address by Keith Vaz, Labour Member of Parliament, whose country of heritage is Goa. He pleaded for "a greater degree of democracy" in the Catholic Church, as in society as a whole, quoting a Punjabi proverb: "The voice of the people is the drum of God."

From the lecture hall the delegates processed with song to the chapel, entering to the resounding African hymn "We are marching in the light of God". Bishop Patrick Kalilombe presided in a striking African chasuble. The music of this mass will be one of the treasured memories of the Congress. At times the congregation joined and lifted hands, and swayed, clapped and almost danced as they sang. At other times there was complete silence, as the congregation responded with deep reverence to the sacred moments of the mass.

The homily was preached by Revd Tissa Balasuriya who reminded the delegates that, "There are many in our countries who would, in spite of all your sufferings, like to be in your place, so in a certain sense you are also a privileged lot." And so "the fight against racism is only one struggle. There are many more. We have to struggle against sexism – for the rights of women; against the class system – where the poor are marginalized, even in this country; against the destruction of nature that is taking place; but I would say much more even, against this world society that has been set up, based on the principles of the accumulation of power, of money, and supported by the rich countries."

After a buffet supper, a small group met to assemble the different recommendations for action that had come from the workshops, and to edit them into a coherent Charter. They worked till the early hours. While this was going on, the other participants met for an uproarious social evening. The guitarists who had played at mass cajoled members of every nationality represented to come forward and either sing a song or do a dance. It was a unique cultural experience.

Sunday was devoted to discussing and perfecting the Charter. And at last the participants left. As one girl had pointed out over a drink in the bar on Friday evening, people were not here just for themselves, but for all the black people back in the parishes: they must return to spread their news and to communicate their new vision.[6]

Reflection

Often in the first world, the educated, middle classes seem more readily conscientized, while the working classes tend to be associated with a more conservative form of thought and devotion. This is a difference that is often noted about the first world as compared with the third world, where the opposite seems to happen. In this Congress, however, it is really the people at the bottom of our society who are coming up with the creativity and determination of a base-community style of Church. Of course the role of pastoral agents is, as ever, very important: the inspiring speeches of black theologians and professionals focus the people's aspirations. Yet it is the people's experience that is the starting point, and it is the people who cry "yes, yes" from their hearts to the way their hopes and feelings are articulated.

Obviously the Congress as such was not a base community. But some of the groups represented could perhaps be called embryonic base communities – groups that meet within a city or deanery or diocese, like the Caribbean chaplaincy, or the Asian chaplaincy. Many of the participants, however, did not come as representatives of organized groups, but simply as one or two individuals representing their diocese.

Often, when people come together for a residential event or conference, the spirit of basic Christian community blows powerfully through the proceedings, as happened on this occasion. If we go through the pastoral cycle, we can find every stage richly represented.

The delegates brought with them their own individual and shared *experiences* of marginalization. They expressed personal stories in the safety of the workshops groups, and Leela Ramdeen gathered together the feelings of all when she said, "We have uttered our cries of pain and frustration for years."

But it was not just a session for moaning, for there was also *social analysis* of the injustice. There was awareness of the dangers of tokenism, for example, by those who did not want to take part in the offertory procession, "as though all were well, until some of the underlying issues of racism were looked at". And there was talk, especially in Tissa Balasuriya's sermon, of the worldwide issues of injustice and poverty, of which racial discrimination in Britain is only one small part.

Theological reflection was expressed in Leela's opening words, when she said the issue was one of touching "the Christ that is in each of us". And it was fed by a contextual reading of scripture, as people pondered the conversion of Cornelius, or Jesus' meeting with the Samaritan woman.

From the start, a high priority was placed on *action*. "These words will lack real weight," Leela said, quoting Paul VI, "unless they are accompanied . . . by effective action." Many practical suggestions emerged, and delegates returned home with the missionary task of communicating the vision to all the black people back in the parishes.

Along with this went an attitude in which black people were no longer to be passive, but became themselves the subjects. Those who were once slaves were now rising "out of the huts of history's shame". No longer were white people to speak and act on behalf of their black brothers and sisters, for "they cannot talk for us . . . there is a word which only you can say". Or, in the words of the Punjabi proverb: "The voice of the people is the drum of God." Innumerable black people found their voice at the Congress, who in other settings before then would have remained silent.

The whole Congress breathed a spirit of *celebration*: there was an outstanding liturgy, in which people practically danced in their places, while the cultural evening, with songs from all over the globe, was a riotous celebration of pride in the many heritages and cultures.

Finally we can comment on the commitment to unity: "one Lord, one world and one Church". Truly in these circumstances we can see how much it matters that a group do not break away in their disillusionment, but act out of a deep internal conviction that they are the Church: "I'm in and I'm not coming out."

It is through experiences of Christian events like these – the women's Holy Week liturgy, or the Congress of Black Catholics, or many other examples all over the first world too numerous to mention – that we begin to experience what the Church should be like, and could be like. To participate in such groups is already to experience something of a base-community style of celebrating our faith. Each such experience brings closer the day when the Church will be transformed in each of its basic cells to a lay-centred Church, faithful to the basics of Christianity, and living out an option for the poor and marginalized of the world.

Chapter 4

STARTING FROM THE PARISH:

El Salvador and Negros

The last chapter reminded us that forming base communities is not the only task in hand. We can move forwards towards a new experience of Church in many other ways: there are so many groups in which Christians meet, apart from the basic Christian community, properly so called.

But if we are to reach all Christians, and not just the elite of activists who are in touch with progressive networks, then sooner or later we have to meet the challenge of how to bring the new way of being Church to the ordinary person in the pew – the person who is not on the circuit of conferences, who is not a member of justice and peace groups, and who is probably not the sort of person who reads books. How do we bring the good news to those who are least in touch with it?

We can only hope to reach the ordinary Christian if we attempt the task of transforming the parish system. Even if church attendance is on a rapid decline, that is still where the great mass of ordinary Christians are to be found, if they are to be found anywhere. And the parish system does provide a network that takes the Gospel everywhere: throughout the city, throughout the country, throughout the world.

Unfortunately, parish work has become very unfashionable. In many religious orders, for example, you will find the bright young priests choosing to work in retreat houses or conference centres or theological colleges, and leaving the tired old men, who have run out of ideas, to keep the parishes going. Many people have come to regard the parish as a dead end – a matter of keeping a decaying show ticking over until it finally conks out.

Not only is this a missed opportunity, but it is unfair on all the thousands of ordinary parishioners who still turn up Sunday after Sunday, and wish their church were more lively. If option for the poor means anything in the first world, it must include a massive shift of resources into parish work. The aim of course is not to keep a dying structure staggering on, but to transform it out of all recognition, in what José Marins calls "open heart surgery".

The parish is not the only possible starting point. Chapters 7, 8 and 9 will look at ways of starting basic Christian community outside of the parish, from "the street" – where there are fewer conventional expectations to challenge, but where there are also years of preliminary evangelizing to be done. But the parish still remains one of the best starting points – because that is where most Christians are to be found, and because that is where reform is urgently needed, as the falling numbers prove.

This chapter and the following two will look in some detail at four specific localities – in El Salvador, the Philippines, England and the USA. This spread of continents demonstrates that wherever in the world we are, the task remains fundamentally the same. Turning a parish into a community of communities may require years of hard work, but it can be done.

El Salvador

First we look at a couple of extracts from the book *Death and Life in Morazán*, by Maria Lopez Vigil, in which the Belgian priest Rogelio Ponseele describes his early work in building up base communities within the parish of Zacamil.

I left Belgium in 1970. I had been a priest in Europe for five years. I knew nothing about Latin America, I knew nothing about anything. I was an immature and extremely timid person. From Belgium to Panama, fifteen days by sea. In Panama I spent a month in the parish of San Miguelito, where they were working with the "God's Family" method. It was a method of pastoral work I was unfamiliar with. I enjoyed the experience. Part of the work was consciousness-raising. We were trying to build up the Church by forming base groups conscious of what their Christian commitment really meant. Various US priests were working in the area with this method. And various pastoral workers came there from all over Central America to learn it.

I arrived in El Salvador on 6 April and went to Zacamil, a district of multi-occupied dwellings on the outskirts of the capital, which is where the bishop had sent Pedro and me. But we did not confine ourselves to Zacamil. We also began working in other districts on the outskirts of San Salvador. Pedro said to me:

"Rogelio, we've got to start work. Let's go and see."

The first thing was to visit people at home. House by house. People were surprised by these visits. They weren't used to the priest going from door to door. They were used to the priest sitting in the parish office noting down masses and baptisms.[1]

When we arrived at Zacamil we found ourselves with a problem which for me was a blessing in disguise: there was no chapel. It didn't bother us much and we met in people's houses to celebrate mass. The work we began was simple. We followed the San Miguelito method. After making home visits and getting to know people well and making friends, we invited those who wanted to do so to form a Christian group. We met with these groups once a week and took each of them through a short course of ten talks. Each of the little groups consisted of from ten to fifteen people. At the end of the ten talks we invited them to go on to something else, a conference. First, though, we did the house-to-house visits and it was only after a year or so that we set up the short courses and the conferences. We always spoke about what was going on in the country and in their lives and in the lives of the people in the Bible, all together. We had considerable success with this method, and got a lot of people to the meetings.[2]

A good complement to those passages is the account from the moving little book, *Faith of a People*, about base communities in El Salvador. Here is an edited version of Pablo Galdámez's account of how the base communities began:

There has to be somebody to call the others in God's name, somebody to say what's happening, somebody to open the door so that the last – who, for Jesus, are the first – can come into the Church, which is the community and not just a building. This is how our communities began – by calling people to congregate, inviting them to come together. The invitees multiplied and became doorkeepers themselves. Andrew called Peter, Philip called Nathanael.

It was a great miracle to see a scattered people come together again. We were beginning to be *one* people. Everywhere little groups were forming, becoming communities. The Gospel was the book from which the communities learned who they were, and from which they learned the reality of the situation in which they lived.

In my parish, the first group was formed one Sunday at the homily. We were having a dialogue on the gospel and were looking for a path to follow. We were looking for answers. We were even looking for questions. This collective homily annoyed some, I remember. One gentleman stood up and said, "Please, don't mix politics and mass!"

But when mass was over some of the congregation stayed to talk. And that's when things got started. We had to get together more often, we said. We had to train, we had to learn some answers. We had to learn to "give an account of our hope" (1 Peter 3:15). Suddenly there was the offer of a house to meet in, and I had my first base group.

A friend of Father Chepe's, a person who worked in a co-op, started meeting with some fellow workers of his. A newly married couple found out about our groups and offered their home as the "synagogue". A nun assigned to social work near the parish took charge of another group. On the south side was a slum we hardly knew about. A member of our community, who worked in a clinic, discovered it and started a little group there. In the slum next to us lived a boy who worked at the university. He started getting people together there. Another group started working twenty kilometers from the parish, directed by a member of our own community. A sister who worked fifty kilometers from the capital got together with a few young people there and started some more communities. The project mushroomed.

With God's Word in hand, we tried to find answers to our problems, and we learned where to find the will of God so that we could keep moving ahead. One who can read life can easily discover the key to holy scripture, with all those living stories of a people on its way to freedom. Another place to read the will of God is in the Christian community. In our group meetings we discovered trails leading to signs of God. And finally in the poor. They are the best book when it comes to knowing what God wants. We only had to keep asking ourselves, "What are we doing? Does it help the poor or not?" And if it did, we kept it up.

In those slums, where there were so many limitations, we didn't get up every day in the same mood. We always needed somebody to keep pushing us along the road. Week after week, meetings. Week after week, community building. "But who'll look after the kids?" Or, "What'll we do with Gram?" Or, "I haven't got time right now." There was always some little obstacle we could use as a pretext for inertia.

And so, an "order of acolytes" sprang up in our communities. Some watched the kids during the meetings, others helped members finish their work so they could come on time, still others took chairs or glasses to the poorest hovels so there couldn't be any excuses. And when people were embarrassed to have the meeting in their shack because the roof leaked and the community would get wet, there was still a way to have a meeting. We fixed the neighbour's roof.[3]

Reflection

These vivid stories from El Salvador prompt a number of reflections. First, from Rogelio's story, we can see what a great influence one place can have on others, in terms of a pastoral method that is worth copying. San Miguelito of Panama was not just a flowering tree by itself: its seeds were borne on the wind not only to El Salvador but all over Central America, so that the work reproduced itself many times over.

And since the essence of the work was visiting and listening, and only then responding, there was no question of transplanting a foreign shrub, for in every patch of soil the plant would grow differently. In the words of Rogelio's colleague Pedro, "We've got to start work," means "Let's go and see." It is interesting also to know that the priests working in San Miguelito were from the USA – from Chicago in fact – demonstrating yet again that the method of basic Christian communities is universal.

We see also that for priests to work in this manner is to deal a blow to people's expectations of the clergy, and that is so even in the third world, even in a parish with the peculiar advantage (in terms of breaking away from established expectations) of not having a church building. We should not be afraid of challenging the assumptions of the people – they will always come to recognize what is good.

Moving on to *Faith of a People*, we observe the importance of personal invitation in building community: "Andrew called Peter. Philip called Nathanael." And the extraordinarily simple way that it began: "Suddenly there was the offer of a house to meet in, and I had my first base group." For first-world people the process of basic Christian community can seem so difficult, so out-of-reach, so tricky to achieve. And yet here we are reminded that at root it could not be more simple and obvious: the people want to discuss the sermon, and so they meet in someone's house.

We notice, too, how there is a multiplicity of pastoral agents, both lay and religious. There is no sense of awe or hesitation about whether anyone is qualified for the work – it is enough just to have the generosity of time to gather people together and offer hospitality.

Once again we notice that resistance to these moves is found in the third world just as in the first world. "Don't mix politics and mass!" says one, but this is not taken as a dampener, but rather as the start of the discussion, from which everything else flows. To continue that discussion the scriptures are read and interpreted, as living stories, read in the same way as life today is read.

Then comes the acid test of good works. Social morality follows as the night the day, from the fact that people have got to know each other: "And when people were embarrassed to have the meeting in their shack because the roof leaked and the community would get wet, there was still a way to have a meeting. We fixed the neighbour's roof." In all things, there is discernment – a search for the way of God – and the search is a community one, with the option for the poor leading the way like a beacon. "What are we doing? Does it help the poor or not?" And if it did, they kept it up.

Tabugon parish, Negros, the Philippines

In Niall O'Brien's enthralling book, *Revolution from the Heart*, he tells the long story of his life as a priest working in the Philippines and his gradual conversion to basic Christian communities.

The following selections concentrate on his struggle to start base communities in his parish in the village of Tabugon. At first the people seemed to have no interest in the idea, and several attempts to start base communities were a failure. But when the ball was finally set rolling, the process was unstoppable.

The account deserves reading in greater detail as it unfolds throughout Niall O'Brien's book, but I have included these sections to give hope for pastoral agents anywhere in the world, who are trying to establish base communities in parishes where people seem interested in nothing more than private devotion.

Small Christian communities in the barrios and hamlets began to take root. Our three first approaches had failed. Approach one was when the original labour leaders had gone out to the villages and tried to start the communities; that had come to nothing. Approach two was when I and Ciano, a seminarian, had gone to the village; we were received with open arms, the communities were initiated, but soon after we were gone they died out, and we heard no more. Approach three was when two sisters volunteered to concentrate in one barrio. They spent months, most of a year, and when they were finished all they had was a very obedient barrio with lots of songs at worship but no community, because the people were not making their own decisions. . . .

The approach which finally worked was startlingly simple. At a marriage interview or at a funeral I would meet a group from a certain hamlet, the name of which I had hardly heard before. I would say: "Do you want to start a small Christian community?"

"Will you come and say mass for us?"

"No, not yet. Why don't you start your own worship service yourselves?" And I would give them a *panimbahon* book with all the steps for a worship service made out simply. "Now you see the Gospel's here . . . . There are questions after them in which you can apply the Gospel to the problems of your own community. The next step is to list all the sick, the old, and the lonely in your village and start to attend to them. And then of course you can start building a chapel. When everything is going, then call me." [Earlier Niall had attempted to dissuade people from building chapels, but he gave up when it was clear that this was an unshakeable desire that came from the people themselves.]

Months would go by and maybe I would never hear from them again. But sometimes someone would arrive to say that they had started the community, their chapel was built, things were going, and they wanted mass. The seed had fallen on fertile ground.

Then I would say: "Well, first I would like you to have a small seminar on what a Christian community really is."

And out our little team would go to give what amounted to a simple explanation of the five-pointed star, the five essential points of a small Christian community.

Then there would be a group discussion of the passage from Luke's gospel: "I was sent to bring good news to the poor." And sometime later they would have their first mass.

[The five points are:
  1) sharing of time, treasure, talent;
  2) group decision-making;
  3) no injustice;
  4) reconciliation;
  5) prayer together.]

By the time I arrived for the mass they were ready. I made sure I did not leave there without making it clear that being a disciple meant sharing in community. The mass became the celebration of that community. We finished with a community meal for the whole hamlet.

I had gone back to worship as an entry point. People wanted to worship. They made it clear that worship was very important to them. The answer had been to concede it as an entry point, but not a finishing point, to insist from the beginning that worship unaccompanied by community sharing would be a counter-sign – a backward step on the road to discipleship.[4]

By the time I came back in January 1981 the number of communities had grown. [Niall had arrived in the parish and begun his attempts to start communities in 1977.] They had spread up the mountains, across the border and into the next diocese of Dumaguete. . . .

With their growth in number, the communities were able to begin functioning more effectively as mini-parishes – groups of small Christian communities federated together because they are geographically situated together. Each region or mini-parish could now have its own regional justice committee. If a person had a justice problem the procedure would now be as follows, after discussing the matter with the community:

1) Dialogue with the landowner who is doing this to you. If you cannot come to a fair agreement, then:
2) Ask the justice committee of your Christian community to try. If the landowner still does not listen, then:
3) Confront the landowner with all the justice committees of the mini-parish, and only if that fails do you then:
4) Come to the *convento*, where the parish council will deal with it and, if necessary, have recourse to the diocesan legal aid office. If that fails, then:
5) There is still the possibility of active, non-violent pressure through the mobilization of the people.

This was a great improvement on the system we started with, where if the people had problems they brought them straight to the *convento*, so that I was taking on everyone's problems. Now they grew in the process of solving things themselves and I began to realize that the primary purpose of all this was not necessarily to win a particular case but rather to lead the people away from the fatalism, which said the problem could not be solved, or the feudalism, which made it utterly unthinkable to confront the landlord or "big" person with what he or she was doing.[5]

The mini-parishes also had education committees. The idea of these committees was to take the weight off the "centre" and shift it out to the periphery for catechesis of various sorts – for example, the pre-baptism seminars, the health seminars, and eventually catechesis in the schools.

In my early days, catechesis had been the obligation and prerogative of the priest. I took it that way and in Kabankalan had an army of catechists employed by me. I looked after their salaries and arranged with the head teachers about the schedules for teaching. But when I got to Tabugon, I realized I had been going in the wrong direction. If we let it all depend on the priest, when he leaves it all collapses. Making it depend on money ensures that the parish is always strapped for funds and frequently under obligation to those powerful people who provide them. But most of all, by making it depend on outsiders we take away from the people their right to pass on their faith themselves, and to grow in the process. It could not be right, I told myself, that someone has to come all the way from Ireland to ensure the Filipino Christians are going to pass on their faith . . . . No more outside catechists on salaries. Christian communities were to choose the teachers, who would be volunteers, and the *convento* was to facilitate their training. The initial result was, of course, that the number of first communions went down dramatically the first year, and I was embarrassed when fellow priests would ask about the first communions. Then in the second year there was the scare about children being kidnapped. But in the third year the communities realized I was not going to come in and teach the children, and they began to elect and choose their teachers, so that by the fourth year the process was quite independent. Religion class was now organized, negotiated, and taught by the communities themselves.[6]

The parish council was different too. It was not a coterie of comfortable, well-off people from the town making decisions to back their own financial interests. It was not a group of well-meaning leaders from the town, trying to guess what was good for the peasants. It was not a clique of ideologues manipulating the people into what they, having seen the light, saw as the only solution. It was the elected leaders of the outlying Christian communities who were serving their own people and knew exactly what the hopes, fears, and aspirations of their communities were.

Nor did the priest rule alone, apart from the parish council. The sixteen parishes had agreed that the priest should have a core group who would decide with him, or on their own in an emergency when he was away. It had become second nature to me to consult with them. In Brian's case it was the core group who had run the parish when he went home for his last furlough, and it was the wives of the core group who had taken over the parish when he and the core group were put in jail. We priests are usually strong-willed individuals, too strong at times. We all had the problem of learning to share power. It is an art, a discipline, a sacrifice, a heroic act of trust.[7]

But probably the most profound change occurred without me realizing it: a change in myself, a new understanding of what it is to be a disciple of Jesus, and therefore a new understanding of what it means to be a priest. In the early days I had seen myself as a model for the other Christians. I could not live up to that, and for a while I was depressed at my own weakness, but somewhere along the line I realized that I was not the model. I was not meant to be the arch-Christian. There were so many real saints around the communities if I would only open my eyes and see – people like Padot and Arod. My task was to discover them, recognize them, learn from them, and help others to learn from them. I would say to myself, going into a new place: "There are some rare and beautiful plants here. My job is to lift the stones and discover them so that the whole community can share them". . . .

Having finally accepted that I was an instrument and not a source of grace, I could now lie down at night knowing that, in every corner of that mountain parish, the natural goodness of people was being unleashed and blessed; and the idyllic vision of the communities of the Acts of the Apostles was finding some reflection because the sick and the old and the young and the lonely were being cared for. And I remembered that curious gospel passage about John the Baptist. While in prison John had got worried as to whether the Messiah really had come. Had he made a mistake? He sent messengers to ask Jesus whether he really was the Messiah. Jesus did not answer directly, he just said: "Look around you. The blind see, the lame walk, the sick are cured, and the poor have the good news preached to them."[8]

Reflection

It is very hard for a pastoral agent to make three attempts to start base communities, and have them all fail, without losing hope. The great temptation is to say, "Obviously base communities are not suitable for our situation. They belong in Latin America, and cannot be transplanted." And yet once the seed had really taken root, the communities thrived and spread – so much so, that the island of Negros has become one of the world's outstanding examples of base-community development.

It is interesting that Niall was able to begin when people naturally came to him with a felt need of their own – to get married, or to bury the dead. So often in the first world we moan at those who only turn up at church for "hatching, matching and despatching"; and yet Niall turned that into a golden opportunity.

It is interesting, too, that he found a way in through what the people already wanted – having mass said for them, and building their own chapel. It reminds us that we can start at any point on the pastoral cycle, and then work round. Faith feeds into life, and life into faith. It is more respectful to the people, as well as more practicable, to begin with what they know they want, rather than with what they do not yet know that they want. So often in the first world, we find that Catholics will never come to meetings, and only turn up for mass; and yet Niall showed how much could be built on that desire. All we have to do is slowly unravel the full meaning of the eucharistic celebration, making it part of a cycle, with a preparation and an outcome. In the first world, with our readily available, daily masses, we take insufficient care when preparing for the eucharist. And the community needs to take more seriously the final words of the mass: "Go in peace to love and serve the Lord."

It is easy to assent to these principles, but Niall makes them so concrete that the people could not just nod their heads and say "yes, yes", as one would to a sermon. He asks the people to make a list of the sick, old and lonely in their village. The same could be done for a house mass in the first world: "Go and list the sick, old and lonely in your street and start to attend to them. And when that work is under way I will come and say mass in your street." In the next case study, from Abbey Wood, London, we will see almost exactly that method used with great success.

One great fear of the clergy is that the more initiatives they start, the more work they will make for themselves. That is why Niall's rather complex system for dealing with injustices has relevance for the first world. By working up through all the levels – individual, small community, mini-parish, parish and diocese – the people are able to deal with their problems, without adding to the priest's workload. Dealing with the problems at the local level wherever possible is called "subsidiarity".

This principle of independence is carried further in the preparation of children for first communion. One wonders how many priests in the first world would have the nerve to let their first communions plummet for several years, in the hope that the people would take on the responsibility for organizing their own catechesis.

In the organization of the parish council, we are reminded to avoid "well-meaning" middle-class people, "trying to guess" what is good for the workers. Representatives should be truly representative of the people they live among, sharing their needs and expectations.

The core-group principle is important too, so the parish priest has a regular team of advisers and colleagues. He can bounce ideas off them, share the work and the strain with them, battle out policy with them, dream dreams with them, and hear their evaluation of his own performance. It is not easy for a priest to work like this – all his training has been against it. It can be a "heroic act of trust" for him.

Finally, after all the years of community-formation, Niall ends with a beautiful picture of a Gospel-based Church, where all over the parish the sick are cared for and the poor have the Gospel preached to them, and without him needing to lift a finger. Though it has been a huge labour to reorganize his parish into small communities, he can now sleep more peacefully than ever before, knowing that the Church is alive and active, no matter what happens to him. Those who read to the end of the book, and hear how Niall was arrested and imprisoned and finally had to flee the country, will realize just how crucial it was for the local Church to grow in independence in the Philippines.

And yet in the first world, it is crucial in another way. Perhaps our clergy are not in danger of being imprisoned or exiled but their numbers are falling, as more priests die or resign than are ordained. If we can learn from the island of Negros we will realize that a priest-less parish is not a tragedy but a precious opportunity. Only when the people have learnt what it means to be Church, can a priest truly fulfil his role – a role of gathering up and sanctifying that Christian community life in the eucharist.

Chapter 5

STARTING FROM THE PARISH:
Abbey Wood, London

Tony Castle is better known for being a writer[1] than for being a
Catholic priest who, in the late sixties, implemented a remarkable
experiment in what we would now recognize as basic Christian community.

Between 1965 and 1972 Tony was curate in the parish of Abbey
Wood, a working-class area in south-east London. During that time
he started an experiment to divide the parish up into neighbourhood
sections. A "section" as such may not sound very exciting. But Tony
found that the smallness of these local groups held the key to what
Church was all about, for it enabled Catholic parishioners to discover
themselves as Christian community. At the time, few people could
see the significance of what he was doing (beyond the members of the
sections themselves, who were experiencing the fruits). But today it
looks prophetic.

Tony had never heard of basic Christian community until many
years after his own experiment. His thinking, he told me, had only
two sources (though we should add to that – as we will see shortly –
the influence of the gospels themselves). First there was Vatican II,
with its theology of the people of God. Secondly there were the
needs of the parish where he found himself. Trying to implement
Vatican II in his parish – trying to turn a mass-going congregation
into a "people of God" – led him straight to a single conclusion: it
could only happen through the formation of smaller, local Christian
communities.

To illustrate the incomprehension he faced within the diocese,
Tony told me a story about an early meeting with his bishop which
took place in the parish priest's study. "Any problems?" asked the
bishop.

"Well yes, there is something," said Tony. "I don't feel we are doing anything for the people."

"What do you mean?" asked the bishop.

"Look out of the window," said Tony. "There are 10,000 people living out there. Only 400 of them come to mass. The other 9,600 we don't touch. It worries me."

The bishop fidgeted and said, "It worries me too. And now I think it is time for lunch."

But Tony persisted with his worry. He was convinced that the "people of God" could not come into being unless there was community. And that means that people must know each other – something they had singularly failed to do in the Catholic parish, with its supermarket approach to dispensing the sacraments. If the people knew each other, then Christian deeds could follow: the people of God could respond to social problems, could visit the sick, and so on. And if the community was seen to be caring, then others could be drawn in, because, he realized, we can only be drawn by personal contact, from people we know and like.

Tony nurtured the experiment of parish sections for seven years. The parish priest allowed Tony to go ahead, but without any conception of the significance of what was happening. "It all went on around him," Tony said, "without him noticing." Tony admits that "it did take a tremendous amount of work to get it going", but slowly he saw the parish being transformed. One story he told me summed up how small communities – not of friends, but of all the local church-members – had a real effect on neighbourhood relations.

Tony had offered to a typical working-class couple to say mass in their house, and for them to invite all the Catholics in the street to attend. They responded without enthusiasm, saying they must go away and think about it. The next day they rang him and said yes. "We said we had to think about it," they explained, "because you said we had to ask all the Catholics in the Close."

"Oh yes," Tony replied, "that is very important."

"Well," they continued, "the people next door are Catholics, and we have not spoken to them for three years, after a row between our son and theirs, and some difficulty over a damaged fence. So last night my wife and I went round and knocked on their door, and they asked us in, and we have made it up. So now we can have the mass."

"The most wonderful thing," Tony told me, "was that you could actually see people growing before your eyes." They acquired a broader vision of what the Church was. They began to ask fundamental questions, so untypical of working-class Catholics, like "Do we have to wait for the priest?" or "Why can't one of us be ordained?" They changed from timid individuals, muttering, "I couldn't manage that", to leaders, coming up with their own ideas, and developing their own creativity.

Abbey Wood began to have a missionary effect on other parishes. In 1969 a priest called Jeremiah Cronin began an almost identical scheme in Crayford, north Kent, where he was curate (again the parish priest allowed it to go ahead, but was unable to play much part himself). This time lessons could be learnt from Abbey Wood, and some improvements were made, particularly over letting leadership emerge more naturally from the sections. Then they discovered that in south Wimbledon a similar, but independent, experiment had been inaugurated in 1968 by Terence Bucher, in which forty-five house masses – said all over the parish territory in a period of three months – resulted in the formation of thirty-five street groups, all lay run. The three priests were able to compare notes and support each other.

But on 15 August 1972 Tony left Abbey Wood and the priesthood, convinced that he had no vocation for celibacy. For a couple of years before that, he had known that would be the decision he would eventually take, but he stayed on to see the sections grow stronger, and to give them that support that he knew they would need from a priest.

When, in 1990, I talked to Tony about that period twenty or so years back, he bubbled over with excitement at the memory of what he had seen happen. "I really, really believe 100 per cent," he told me, "in its potential for changing the Church." But he added ruefully, "One of the biggest sadnesses of my life, is to see something with so much potential not go anywhere." He had been back recently, however, for a wedding, and was moved to see that something lived on. In particular he was thrilled to find one working-class family, who he remembered as very shy and diffident, playing a leading role in the liturgy, with the husband leading the choir and the daughter writing music for the wedding. "People were still talking," Tony said, "about how good things were back then, and about how little things still continue. But the overall scheme faded, when there was no longer a priest with that vision working among them."

Tony wrote his own account of the experience, working at the report several evenings every week in the first year of his marriage, because he believed that something so important had taken place at Abbey Wood. I now give a large part of that account, which has never before been published, in Tony's own words.

Tony Castle's account

When I first went to Abbey Wood in south-east London, as an assistant priest in May 1965, it was very evident that no sense of community existed among the worshipping Catholics. One of the obvious reasons was the existence of two parallel lines of steel belonging to British Rail, which neatly divides the Abbey Wood parish into two equal halves of approximately 10,000 people. Although both parts of Abbey Wood were, and still are, solidly working-class, those who live in the older, more established part looked down on the new arrivals, who inhabited the Greater London Council estate.

Both halves have their own churches, for a new church had been put up as the estate itself grew. Within two minutes of the last word from the priest on a Sunday, the whole church and its immediate environment was vacant. If the two halves were ever going to be united into one community, if the Sunday mass was to have any claim to being the community at worship, then the very minimum requirement would be that the community members knew one another. This accomplished, we might move on to the objective of helping them to work together and grow in acceptance of one another. But how was this to be accomplished?

I referred the problem to "authority". Receiving little assistance from that quarter, I tried the gospels. When we look carefully at the gospels with this problem in mind, we discover that Christ not only gave us a command to take the Good News out beyond ourselves – he showed us how to do it!

For example, in John's account of the Gospel, chapter 4, we read how one day, Jesus passing through Samaria, stopped at a well there, and appearing to be tired, sent his apostles on an errand. Apparently he wished to be alone. When a woman from a nearby Samaritan town approached the well, Jesus broke social convention and traditional practice by asking her for a drink. Then he launched into a conversation with her. As a result of this seemingly chance encounter, Jesus was invited into the Samaritan town – an opportunity that presumably he had hoped for. He spent several days in the town, talking to people and making new friends.

A closer look at Jesus' method shows it to be both a simple and most efficient one. There are three stages to it. First, he boldly opens a relationship with the woman by asking a little favour of her, then, building on this, he opens a full conversation with her and thus builds a relationship with the woman. The second stage is when the woman goes to her friends and invites them to come and meet Jesus, and with these he opens a relationship. The third stage is when the whole group invites Jesus to come into the town, where, we read, he makes many disciples. Person-to-person contact: the simple and most efficient method of Christ.

Preaching on street corners with a loud hailer, pestering people on their doorsteps, leaving Catholic Truth Society pamphlets on the top seats of red London buses – these and similar methods fail, because they are too impersonal. My own opinion, that mission through community could best be attained through person-to-person contact, became total conviction when, shortly after meditating on the above gospel passage, a providential meeting occurred.

While on holiday with a priest friend we found ourselves sharing a hotel, in foreign parts, with an extremely pleasant middle-aged couple. After three days and several meals together, it transpired that the gentleman was the manager of a very famous London First Division football club. By the end of the two-week holiday the four of us had become firm friends. I was so impressed by the personality and character of the manager, that on my return home I discovered that I had become a firm supporter of his team.

The wonder of this conversion is only properly understood if one is aware that, previous to the holiday, I had absolutely no interest whatever in football, especially First Division football. I now read every Saturday evening or Sunday morning the news report of the Saturday fixture and follow the fortunes of the club with an enthusiasm that I never dreamt of! Occasionally I make the pilgrimage to the London ground and express my enthusiasm vocally. I am, without doubt, a convert to professional football. While on holiday, Ron Greenwood, manager of West Ham, never once voluntarily spoke about the club or the players, in fact he had been reluctant at first to reveal what his work was. It was because of his character and personality, not because of any attempt at "selling" his club, that I became interested in West Ham.

As in the gospel cited above, so in this example, conversion came and influence spread through person-to-person contact. The story did not end with a return from holiday! Shortly after my return I went to see my parents, and among other things, told them about meeting the manager of West Ham. More recently I have discovered that my parents now read the newspaper reports on West Ham's matches, and count themselves as supporters too!

Bringing parishioners together to form a real outward-looking Christian community; reaching out to the non-committed to share Christ with them; how were these two absolutely vital needs to be met? Person-to-person contact certainly, but how?

In the course of deep and long conversation with Mary Burgess, one of the stalwart "mums" of the inner circle of parish helpers at Abbey Wood, an idea was born. Mary said, "Everything is too big. Let's divide the whole parish up into smaller areas. Then in each area there will be genuine opportunity for person-to-person contact. When the parts are communities, the whole will naturally follow." While the subsequent working out and following through of action was done by myself, the original idea was offered by Mary.

Late in 1967, with the aid of the natural boundaries in the locality – the railway line, the allotments, the main roads, etc. – the whole area was divided into twelve parts, or, as they came to be called, "sections". This meant that there were approximately thirty to thirty-five addresses of known Catholics in each section. Nearly two-thirds of these were non-practising Catholics.

Having made the divisions, the next task was to introduce the idea to the Catholics that worshipped regularly. The idea of linking Christianity to a concern for "community" had never struck them, although those on the estate who had originated from Poplar, Stepney and North Woolwich spoke frequently of "the good old days," when there was a wonderful spirit of sharing in those overcrowded areas. They had found that material betterment on the council estate could bring isolation and depression.

The parish priest "did not mind" about the scheme, for it was put to him that the sections would provide a very easy way of delivering the offertory envelopes – one of his principal concerns. Once he was assured that the football pool would not suffer in any way, and covenant schemes and bingo were not in jeopardy, he was happy to let the curate get on with it, while he continued his somewhat independent life.

A series of Sunday sermons was launched, by one of the priests, linking the concept of community with the sacraments. A sheet was put together explaining very simply the need for sections on one side and giving the actual details of the twelve divisions on the reverse. These sheets were distributed at every possible opportunity, especially at two parish meetings called to explain the new parish structure. The response to these meetings was typically very poor, but this was expected. In order to start using the sections immediately, while explaining their purpose, two meetings were arranged in each of the new sections, in selected homes.

The delivery of the invitation letters, sent to every known Catholic living in the section, was entrusted to volunteers from the local church school. The response was again not very encouraging, only the inner-circle few who, in the main, already knew one another, turned out to these meetings in the home. However, this really did not matter too much, because it would have been foolish to have ploughed ahead before there was basic understanding among the regulars, about what the "section system" was setting out to achieve and the importance of working hard to achieve it. For the very first time, many of these working-class parishioners started to understand what the phrases "the people of God" and "we are the Church" – which they had heard in use at Sunday mass – really meant.

During this initial round of house meetings, the fundamental question of communication between the priests' house and the sections was raised time and again. This became linked with the concept of section leadership. In Abbey Wood, the decision was taken to appoint leaders, mainly to get the distribution of offertory envelopes working effectively, this being the justification for the scheme offered to the parish priest. This pressure to placate the PP resulted in an unwise decision for the scheme as a whole, as events proved. (The Crayford parish in Kent, who adopted the idea a year later, learnt from the Abbey Wood experience and first allowed a little committee to develop in the section before moving to the appointment of a suitable section leader.)

In February 1968, when this scheme was being introduced, house masses were unknown in the parish. The next step in the development of our project was the systematic use of the eucharist in the home to build community. There was a certain amount of uneasiness at the first suggestion of mass in the home, but this was quickly dispelled when priest and people alike became accustomed to the idea. Immediately the introductory meetings had been completed the house masses began.

To avoid any possible accusation of preferential treatment, the first twelve masses – two each week, taking the sections in turn – were said in the homes of the housebound and aged, who could be found in all the sections. Mrs Maynard's one-bedroom flat was the home in which the first mass was said – to be followed by hundreds of others. The ninety-two-year-old invalid's joy at being present at mass, after seven years, and meeting fourteen of her neighbours was quite indescribable. "Isn't it wonderful", the lonely old lady said, "fancy them bothering to come and see me in my home". Many of the visitors that evening started popping in to see her on a regular basis. This cheered, what proved to be, the last six months of her life.

After each of the first twelve masses the new experiment was explained and the implications were discussed. At the same time a list of those who would like to have mass in the home in the future was drawn up. Where meetings had failed abysmally, house masses drew not only the practising Catholics, but very many of the lapsed and not a few interested neighbours who boasted no Church allegiance. To begin with, most of those who came were total strangers to one another. This new type of response was more due to the doorstep invitations from the section leaders than the letters of invitation that also poured out from the priests' house.

The section leaders could see three very necessary phases in the development of the new parish structure. The first phase, which we were then engaged upon, was the introduction of practising Catholics to one another and encouragement of sound relationships between them.

The second phase was the most positive approach to all those Catholics who had lapsed from the practice of their religion, to give them the opportunity of entering into the makings of a community that had resulted from the first phase. (The key phrase throughout these years was "to provide the opportunity", for everyone realized that the duty we had was to provide the opportunity for others to respond, we could do no more.)

Phase three was the opening up of each section's activities to all those who lived in that area, no matter what their beliefs. We hoped that by then the social service which was beginning to develop in most sections would be providing a realistic service to the sick and needy of Abbey Wood.

I have so far failed to mention that two interesting developments occurred as the first year progressed. They were both instigated by the section leaders themselves. The first was the development of section social life. One section discovered that it had a fair number of young mothers with young children, who felt isolated and lonely. For them the section arranged coffee mornings. The idea spread to other sections. Section Twelve, I remember, was the first to arrange an outing to a West End show for its members. That idea, too, caught on among the sections, although some preferred an evening's journey to a country pub or a weekend excursion to the coast.

The second development was the founding of section newsletters, which proved to be a short-lived experiment in the four sections that tried it. *Link, Two-Time* and the others only survived a year or two, but in that short time they contributed to the build up of the community in their respective sections. Financed by the funds raised at the coffee mornings, they were delivered free to all section members and brought many people in touch with the activities of the section and the parish.

After eighteen months, two of the sections became leaderless, because the men who had been asked to take on this work for one reason or another felt unequal to what the position demanded of them. After a short while they were ably replaced by two women leaders who "emerged" from the meetings and activities within the sections.

About this time the leaders asked for some kind of training. As some of them were on shift work the best time to meet for a training session was clearly Sunday afternoon. A weekly training meeting – on top of their family and section commitments – seemed much too demanding, so we all agreed upon six sessions of two hours each, on alternate Sundays. With the aid of two of the leaders I put together a training programme which owed much to the "See-Judge-Act" method of training. The course proved successful. Priest and leaders learnt from one another during it, and grew in their mutual understanding of what working for "community" demanded of them and the benefits it brought. (Two years later the leaders asked for another course, which also proved beneficial.)

One of the more obvious results of the first training session was the development, in most sections, of section committees. The constitution of each committee depended upon the needs of the section, the number and quality of the volunteers available, and the personality of the leader.

When the parish council became a reality, in the second year of the parish experiment, the whole atmosphere within the parish had definitely altered for the better. The election of councillors took place in and through the sections, and the section leaders were considered, like the priest, to be "ex officio" members of the Parish Pastoral Council.

The third year of the experiment was marked by the launching of a good-neighbour scheme. At first only on the estate, it later spread throughout the whole of Abbey Wood. It was conducted completely through the organization of each section: the section leader and his (or her) helpers took responsibility for helping or finding help for the handicapped and housebound. Holidays for old people were arranged and financed in co-operation with the local authorities.

This good-neighbour scheme worked in complete co-operation with the Anglican church, especially on the estate, where the vicar rearranged his parish to fit in with the six sections of the estate. (Two Anglican parishes are incorporated in the area served by the Catholic parish of Abbey Wood.)

The transformation of the parish into something like an outward-looking Christian community was gradual. It would be dishonest to give the impression that the experiment went like clockwork and that there were not setbacks and difficulties. Apathy and misunderstanding, especially at the very beginning, seemed a dead weight which would never be lifted – yet much of it was, eventually. The ingrained need to refer everything back to "Father", before taking any action, took some shifting too. There was also a constant need to remind the laity "why sections". There was the danger that they might become merely useful finance-gathering units – a good way to organize people to work for the Christmas bazaar!

Sometimes people wanted to amalgamate neighbouring sections in order to make events in individual sections more "successful". This meant using the people to be counted on in each of the sections, rather than making the effort to call upon and involve the less committed. These and other temptations and difficulties were fought through occasional campaigns, like "Think Week" and "Area-wise".

Although there was the big disappointment in the total lack of interest shown by the diocesan authorities (although they were well aware of the existence of experiments taking place in the Abbey Wood parish) there was plenty of compensation to be found in the tremendous "growth" in Christian maturity among the section leaders, their helpers and the parish councillors.

The sense of responsibility spread to the young people who, allowed to organize their own Parish Youth Council, were given responsibility for the affairs of parishioners under the age of twenty-five. This included the organization of youth vigils, youth masses, weekends away and other events to further the social and spiritual well-being of the parish young folk.[2]

Reflection

I have used an example from a parish in the sixties for good reason. It is not by any means intended to imply that nothing of this kind has happened since then: on the contrary, we hear continually of new experiments in turning the parish into a community of communities from all over the world. Rather, it illustrates how universally applicable is the concept of basic Christian communities. Back in 1965 – three years before Medellín first put a name to this phenomenon in

Latin America – a parallel development was already happening in Britain. The fact that it was called "sections" rather than base communities is of no relevance. What matters is that this is a way of rediscovering what it means to be Church, that can pop up at any time, in any part of the world, among people of any culture.

What are my reasons for identifying the Abbey Wood experiment with the basic ecclesial communities we have observed from the third world? They are many. We can notice that, just as in Latin America, what happened at Abbey Wood was a direct response to Vatican II, an attempt to apply the insights of the Council to the local situation. We can notice in both cases that the concept of the "people" was central – in Abbey Wood expressed particularly through the conciliar phrase "the people of God". In both settings it was basic to recentre around a vision of Church as people, not as building.

We see at Abbey Wood, as in the third world, that the new development occurs not among a social or intellectual elite, but among the ordinary working-class Christians. We see that in order to achieve this – to bring in all the people and renew the experience of Church for everyone, not just for a few advanced "progressives" – Tony Castle systematically divided up the map of the parish, using natural boundaries, just as third-world base communities are divided up according to locality.

Again, as in the third world, we see the essential importance of the pastoral agent, and particularly of the clergy, in launching the idea and promoting the new structure at parish level. The active encouragement of a priest proves to be the crucial factor, even when the priest is only the curate of the parish and when the bishop is uncomprehending and uninterested. The support of a bishop would have been appreciated, and would have helped to communicate the idea to others, but the lack of that support did not inhibit the development. But we see also the importance of dynamic and committed laity taking a leadership role within each section, becoming themselves pastoral agents.

We see the importance of starting where people are and with what they want. In this case the experiment began to get under way with masses, not with meetings, because that was what people wanted. Having begun there, however, the people were led far beyond, to a new vision of social responsibility. You can start at any point on the pastoral cycle, as long as the process then continues in a circular direction.

We see again the importance of personal invitation, so that even a letter from the priest is less effective than a doorstep invitation from a near neighbour. In this way, the sections began at an early date to have a missionary dimension.

We see also how the scriptures were beginning to be used, and applied to the practice of the local sections, in a way that was new for Catholics at that time.

We see an option for the poor being exercised, as the sections focus on the needy of the area – the elderly, the lonely, the sick, the disabled. We see how this concern is exercised not just for Catholics but for anyone in the locality. And we see the beginnings of co-operation with Christians of other denominations in this social caring.

We see the importance of relaxation and social get-togethers in the building of community – anything from a drink in the pub to a West End show.

We see how the small communities lead inevitably to a more serious understanding of what it means to be a eucharistic community: we cannot attend mass together without setting aside feuds, and greeting each other as sisters and brothers. We see how deeper theological questions arise among very ordinary people, as they begin to work out what ministries in the Church are for. We see how a request for leadership training naturally arises, and how the "See-Judge-Act" method is used as a part of that training. We see a growth in mutual responsibility, even among the young people.

Overall, the principle is a clear and simple one. If the Church is to be a community, it must be small. If the community is to be for everyone, it must be local. From these two points, everything else naturally follows. And though there was a struggle, with apathy and misunderstanding seeming at first like an unliftable weight, persistent work over a period of years did lift it, and a new way of being Church was born.

Chapter 6

STARTING FROM THE PARISH:
Lakewood, Colorado

From England in the sixties we travel to the United States in the seventies, where Richard Ling, a Catholic priest of the diocese of Denver, developed a strikingly similar experiment in the parish of Christ on the Mountain. Of course he knew nothing of Tony Castle's work at Abbey Wood, but he did have some knowledge of the existence of third-world base communities at the date when he began, in 1975.

Dick has written his own account of his experience at Christ on the Mountain.[1] His story, he says, is one "of imagining a different kind of Catholic Church, a Church with a different kind of structure that enables it to be a Church of greater compassion, dialogue, equality, mutual empowerment, and solidarity with people, especially the poor and marginal people of the earth".

After twenty-seven years in pastoral ministry, he says, "I am convinced that trying to improve the traditional parish model – one I have experienced first hand in ten different parishes – is a sadly misdirected effort, like putting band-aids on cancer patients. Spending long days attempting to renew or polish the customary parish approach is as wise as trying to teach a one-winged bird to fly." And so he became convinced that "the structure, not the veneer, of the Church must change", so as to become "a Church of compassionate mutuality, wherein the rich and the poor will minister with and to one another in compassion for a world larger than the Church".

Dick Ling went as pastor[2] to a new suburban parish in Lakewood, Colorado, in 1975. Originally this was called "Green Mountain parish", though it later changed its name to "Christ on the Mountain". He describes the parish as "relatively affluent" and "predominantly Anglo", with "a few who were poor". The experiment is therefore of considerable interest in showing how small ecclesial communities can operate in a middle-class culture. As I have already argued, though there is an option for the poor built into the concept of basic ecclesial community, this does not mean that every community must itself be poor, for ultimately the hope is that the communities will develop all over the Church.

Dick and his parish team, of eight laity and a pastoral associate, hammered out a "Parish Concept" as a framework for their pastoral strategy. "Fundamentally, our overall goal was to develop a sense of community at two different extremes: to strive for a large, profound sense of unified community at the 'assembly' level (weekend mass) while we also created and developed a sense of an *interrelated and caring* community at the neighbourhood level." The changes are structural and radical, but we can see at the same time that they belong to a deeper understanding of what a parish should be, not to a rejection of the parish. Note that though he rejects "the traditional parish model" and "the customary parish approach", he does not reject the parish as such.

These caring, neighbourhood communities were originally called "base communities". But Dick now feels the term "base communities" is unsuitable, because "base" holds connotations from a third-world context which are "inappropriate in the US". Later they were called "ACTION communities", standing for Awareness, Commitment and Transformation Involving Our Neighbourhood. We can see at once from this title that an ACTION community was based on what we have been accustomed to call the pastoral cycle, or "See-Judge-Act" principle.

Other terms Dick uses are "small Christian communities" (which we may recall is the usage in most parts of Africa), "small church communities" and "small ecclesial communities". An ACTION community is one form of small ecclesial community – the form that developed in Christ on the Mountain parish. But whatever the term, we can clearly recognize in what he describes the authentic essence of what has been called in this book basic ecclesial community.

As Dick describes what happened in his parish, we can feel that air of excitement which so often accompanies a base community project – a sense that the Church is being reborn.

We prayed and walked together on this wonderful adventure, relishing the widespread co-operation of parishioners, parish council and staff. Team experiences were in themselves a model of what we wanted to foster in the neighbourhood church communities. Our many planning meetings, evenings of facilitating the small groups, and training their ministers remain my fondest example of what it means to "be a priest" in dialogue with equals enabling others in a new kind of Church.

The first contacts

Within a few months of becoming pastor, Dick took a house-to-house survey of the entire parish, and he marked every Catholic household with a pin on a huge map. Then the area was broken down as follows. The parish was divided into seven large "districts". Each district was divided into four "neighbourhoods". Each neighbourhood was divided into six "communities". And each community would contain approximately six households.

One of the functions of the districts was to provide a representative for the parish council, which was involved from the beginning in discussing and approving the Parish Concept. And one of the functions of the neighbourhoods was to be a work area for tasks like census-taking. But the primary focus of pastoral activity fell on the communities. This whole secretarial process of making maps and sticking in pins turned out to be a mammoth task, even with many volunteers. It lasted two years.

The next step was more intensive door-to-door visiting by Dick within a selected area. This meant that community-forming began with evangelization, as Dick went from house to house to get an idea of people's religious positions and needs. (He explains that he was the one to visit because "no one else would do it", although later on laity became willing to take it on.) Most of the visiting had to be done in the evenings to find people at home. Based on the information Dick received at the door, together with information about the more active parishioners that was already available, he classified each household according to whether they were active church-goers, friendly or alienated. Each category had a different coloured pin on the parish map.

The initial visit was followed up by a letter, sent to all the Catholic households, saying that the parish was trying to live Christianity in a way that made sense to ordinary people, and that he hoped they would consider being a part of this process. Next, Dick personally telephoned each household to say that "our laity and I had worked out what we thought was a wonderful way of living our Christianity in a more real way, six days a week". If they were not already church-goers, Dick asked if he might call by some evening, and often he managed to join them for a meal. By the time he had refined his approach, he was getting four out of five of the inactive Catholics to accept this offer of a visit. He would try to spend as much time as possible listening to people's bad experiences of the Church in the past, but another primary purpose of his visit was to persuade them to come to an evening when the Parish Concept would be explained. Again, four out of five of those visited agreed to come to this evening, even after Dick had explained it would be the first of a four-week process.

Although Dick was making these visits himself, the whole team was involved in evaluating the procedure and in discussing how to respond sensitively so as to welcome without pressurizing. The final outcome was that 95 per cent of the practising Catholics, and about 65 per cent of the lapsed, came to the four evenings of community-building, and in fact remained part of the ACTION communities. We have to realize that Dick must have had a gift of sensitivity to be able to get the results he records. The same method carried out by a more clumsy person could yield very different results; and in a different sort of area, where people are less confident, a more grad-ual, gentle build up might be needed. But the basic principle of personal contact made through house-to-house visiting remains of crucial value in every context.

The programme of four meetings

Before the meetings actually started, the team were looking for at least three households which were willing to meet, although usually they had five or six, and at least two households should be already active in their faith. Meeting these criteria was not difficult with the help of the parish map, because they could always group a potential

ACTION community together from looking at the coloured pins.

The meeting was to be held in a nearby home of a church-going Catholic. Before the first meeting, the team would ring up any other church-going Catholics and help them to be sensitively prepared for a meeting at which lapsed Catholics would be present, who might express anger and resentment against the Church. The meetings would be facilitated by two laity from the team. No meeting lasted longer than an hour and a half.

At the first meeting there would be a welcome, and some "warm-up procedures" to enable people to get to know each other. Then there was a reading of scripture and a prayer. Next a home-produced tape and slide show would be presented, on the theme of community, which included local scenes and pictures of some of the team. In the following discussion, the team leaders "tried to say little or nothing, encouraging the participants to talk freely about their attitudes toward the Church, its hospitality and concern for others, etc." The evening finished with scripture and prayer again. Finally there was fifteen minutes for relaxed socializing over simple refreshments.

Approximately 80 per cent of the people who came to the first meeting would turn up at the second, which was on the Parish Concept and how it was relevant to the kind of issues they had been discussing on the function of community. After that, Dick said, "I cannot recall any person ever coming to the first two evenings and then dropping out for either the third or the fourth evenings." The format of the meetings followed the same pattern as the first week – scripture, spontaneous prayer, and then the theme of the week, ending again with scripture, prayer and refreshments.

The second meeting encouraged questions like: "Why only six households in a community?" "What about spouses from other denominations?" "What about others in the same neighbourhood?" This second meeting was followed up with sending a prayer card, which listed the names and addresses of all the Catholic households in the new ACTION community (even those who had chosen not to attend the sessions), a little map with the boundaries marked, the names and phone numbers of the team, and a simple prayer.

At the same time, those marginal Catholics who had been invited but had not responded received a friendly and respectful letter, so that they would not be left with the sense that there was now yet another Catholic activity from which they felt alienated, and this often led to a positive response.

The third evening was devoted to explaining six ministries that were needed in a community, described more fully below. "There was always a lot of interest and excitement about what needed to be done in a particular community and who might be the best minister for a particular responsibility." No decisions were made at this third meeting, but people took home a sheet that outlined the different ministries.

It may seem early to be getting such a response, but in practice the team found that:

> . . .the third session was often our most wonderfully emotional evening. . . . Marginal Catholics would share some deep feelings of anger or disappointment about their "old Catholic Church". Then, sometimes with tears and a great sense of relief, they would admit that the sessions (and especially the practicality of the six ministries) had helped them see that the Catholic Church was changing very much for the better, and that they were delighted to "come home again".

Sometimes the return was to the ACTION community rather than to mass-going, and parish worship came as a later step.

Dick himself always attended the fourth meeting, even if he had not been at the others. The meeting was devoted to discussing who would take which ministry: generally there was common agreement about who was suitable for what and who would like to do what. The chief concern of the team was to ensure that the administration ministry was not taken by a dominating personality. It was also made clear that you did not have to take on a ministry to belong to the ACTION community, and sometimes not all the ministries were covered, but for the most part it more or less worked out.

Then there was a little ritual of commitment. "We deliberately avoided the eucharist, not only because of mixed-religion marriages within the ACTION communities, but because we wanted to set a mood which affirmed the value of simple rites in the communities." Signatures were written on a covenant card, there was a scripture reading, a short homily by Dick, the use of salt as a biblical symbol, and the formal inauguration of the community, ending "with unusually expressive embraces".

> These profoundly moving fourth evenings, were then, and remain to this day, the most satisfying and joyful moments of my priestly life. In my first thirteen years of priesthood, I spent so much time working with individuals in non-communal contexts, only to see my labour so frequently frustrated because no on-going community existed to nourish and support the persons after I had begun . . . . The fourth evenings were a partial means to ending a dependency on "Father" and a signal that the core of Catholicism – a sense of community in Christ and the Spirit – was going to exist, flourish, and last.

The ministries

Six ministries were suggested – growth, social events, assistance, transition, stewardship and administration. Through some of these ministries the ACTION communities could function in important ways without the community having to convene for every activity. Administration was presented last, to avoid "the patriarchal tendency to begin with an 'administrative' focus, as if to hint or outright claim that it is the most important one. It is placed last to emphasize its service to the other ministries."

The "growth" ministry covered both worship and religious education, and this minister was given the minimum requirement of gathering the community at least twice a year for a religious education event and at least twice a year for worship. The minister was given help later through training sessions, in knowing what resources were available.

There was also a bi-monthly newsletter, published by the team, which suggested activities and prayer services, such as Thanksgiving table prayers or Advent wreath prayers; and a lot of creative ideas that were coming up through the communities were shared through this newsletter.

The second ministry was "social events", which was one of the easiest jobs to fill. Again, this minister was asked to organize at least two events a year, and also to invite along any Catholics who had declined to come to the four meetings but had responded in a friendly way to the subsequent letter. Birthday parties and camping trips were popular, and there could also be outreach, for example when a block party was arranged for everyone in the immediate neighbourhood.

Two creative ideas in particular turned out to be a great success, and they spread around the communities. One was to "adopt" an elderly resident from a nearby nursing home, who would be brought along for social celebrations on their birthday or for Christmas or Thanksgiving. The other was to organize a "honeymoon weekend" for a local young couple, struggling with the demands of a young family: a collection was taken to send them on a weekend away, around the date of their wedding anniversary, while the members of the ACTION community looked after the baby-sitting.

The third ministry was "assistance" to those in need. This might include house-painting, baby-sitting or house-sitting. It might involve providing a supper casserole for households that were suffering an emergency, like a death in the family. With the benefit of subsequent study of liberation writers, Dick is now convinced that "future training of assistance ministers in ACTION communities must include a dimension of solidarity with the poor on a wider basis".

Fourthly, there was the ministry of "transition", which meant welcoming those who moved into the area and saying goodbye to those who moved out. The welcome was to anyone in the area – not just Catholics.

Fifthly, there was the "stewardship" ministry. This meant meeting once a year with every household and chatting about the sharing of "time, treasure and talent" at a parish level, not just a local level. This was not a popular ministry and was often left unfilled in the community, though there would normally be a stewardship person in the district. Like "assistance", Dick feels that "stewardship" is relevant to option for the poor, with the possibility of opening up a broader worldview. He plans in future that each community be "encouraged to bond itself in solidarity with a base community in the third world".

Finally, there was the ministry of "administration". This meant that the person would be there *ad ministra*, that is "for the ministers", serving all the others in their ministries and keeping an eye on the overall spirit of community. Dick thought of it rather like an "overseer", and he avoided that term only because it is usually applied to bishops. The job included being a contact person with the pastor and the team, discerning the needs of the community, supporting and encouraging the other community ministers, and filling in any gaps of vacant ministries.

After the series of four local meetings was over, anyone who had undertaken a ministry was invited to a three-hour training session at the parish centre. Dick would give a talk on general theological aspects and then people would go into groups according to the ministry they had taken on.

One of the difficult decisions faced by Dick and the parish team was whether to spend time and energy "holding the hands" of newly formed ACTION communities, or to "cut the umbilical cord" and devote time instead to the formation of new communities. After much discussion and heart-searching, they decided on the latter course. "The effect of our decision was bitter-sweet. A few ACTION communities simply withered and continued to function only at the lowest levels." But "most of the ACTION communities took charge of their life and struggled along, sometimes with outstanding experiences, more often with a quiet sense that their life together was developing and making a difference among and beyond them."

As an initial goal, set in the mid-1970s, the team hoped to convert half of the parish into ACTION communities by the year 2000. But as a result of their policy of cutting the cord and moving on, and of the dynamism and enthusiasm that built up, they would have converted the whole parish into communities by 1995, had the process continued at the same rate.

What actually happened was that in 1982 Dick was moved on, seven years after he had arrived. At that time thirty communities had been formed, spread well out, for it was a deliberate policy to start them as far apart from each other as possible. The earliest dozen "never jelled or functioned very well because we tried to cut corners by having all twelve meet together in the parish centre rather than their homes. But in the later, more patient stages of our process, the process went very well." As is the general practice with base communities, evaluation and consequent improvement was always a regular part of the process.

The fate of the communities will surprise few: Dick Ling calls it "the greatest sadness of my life" (almost exactly the words used by Tony Castle, in not dissimilar circumstances). "Before I left, the parish staff, council, and ACTION community team addressed a concerted, serious plea to the archdiocese – send a pastor who will support the Parish Concept and the team. By the time I left, the team was able to function on its own, needing only the basic affirmation and support of the pastor." However, "over a period of a couple of years it became clear that the new pastor had other directions that excluded the Parish Concept." Despite this lack of encouragement, "about half of the ACTION communities still continue to meet and function on their own, reflecting both the basic determination of the people to benefit from the small communities and the soundness of one principle upon which they were built – the ACTION communities were fundamentally lay directed."

But Dick has by no means given up. After a period of academic research, studying other work on small ecclesial communities, he lectures on the topic frequently all over the USA. He is now back as pastor in another parish,[3] where the plan can be implemented all over again, with the benefit of even more experience. Among the changes he would make this time, are more integration of children – a point on which he was out-voted by the team at Christ on the Mountain – and a longer period for the overall preparation and preliminary evangelization. And we have already observed the greater emphasis he would now wish to place on a wider sense of option for the poor.

Reflection

The success of the ACTION communities at Christ on the Mountain parish almost sounds too good to be true, but it does demonstrate how small communities really hold the key to making the Church come alive for people.

In this case, as with Tony Castle's experiment in Abbey Wood, we see how small communities and the larger parish can work together in perfect harmony. Not only is there no hint of a threat to the parish, but the communities enormously enrich what is going on at parish level. The communities were used to gather viewpoints on issues facing the parish council; they were also sources of sponsors for the sacraments of baptism, RCIA[4] and first communion. But the small ecclesial communities are not used to prop up an outdated parish system: the Parish Concept really is a radical change from anything that came before.

The most striking difference between the communities in Abbey Wood and in Christ on the Mountain is that the former began around house masses, whereas the latter "deliberately avoided" the eucharist. There is no contradiction here: it is a matter of different means to the same end. In Abbey Wood the development was to start from what people knew they liked – going to mass. Once they began to form a community they would meet for other activities, apart from the one that originally drew them together. Dick's idea started at the other end. He worked hard at getting people together in the first place, and from the beginning he led them to discover what the community could do without the priest.

There were two respects in which Dick's concept of Christian communities ran counter to what most parishes were trying in terms of small communities. On both I believe his instinct was right, although he has been criticized on these points.

In the first place, the ACTION communities, like Tony Castle's sections, were rigorously neighbourhood-based. People were told which community they belonged to, and could not say "I would rather belong to my friends' community in the next street but one". And so, critics said, people were "forced" into particular communities.

But this way of thinking is odd if we have taken aboard the idea of the base community as the basic cell of the Church. No one complains that they are "forced" into a particular parish or a particular diocese – it just happens to be a fact about where their home is situated. And there is no "forcing" to attend: people are still free to worship in another parish that is not their own, and often do. In the same way, I see no objection in principle to people meeting in a small ecclesial community that is not their own. After all, this is exactly what happens when an external pastoral agent (a priest, or member of a parish team) is present. But the reason why people worship in other parishes is usually because they feel their contributions are unwelcome in their own one, rather than just a desire to be with friends: there should be less need to go outside their own area when a participatory, democratic, local community scheme is working.

Throughout this book I have presented the geographical basis for base communities as something very valuable – as an expression of the universality of the Church, that avoids the limitations of self-selecting groups. Dick Ling's attitude is exactly the same. "Intentional communities", he says – that is, communities that people choose to join, as opposed to neighbourhood communities – run the risk of being "cosy, warm fuzzies", gathering together similar types, so there is an "equality of friends", rather than gathering those who are different for an "equality amid diversity". (I should stress that this is by no means a condemnation of intentional communities, which perform an excellent and much needed function. But it is a different function from that of a basic ecclesial community.)

By contrast, the ACTION communities

> . . . could be blessed with a unity amid a rich mixture of differences: a truck driver, small children, a single-parent household, a divorced person, a wealthy family, an elderly widow, a blended family, teenagers, etc. It was a "catholic" community. . . . In a real, though sometimes minimal way, our ACTION communities were a collaboration of the rich and the poor, the "ins" and the "outs".

But the geographical principle is not an absolute one. Dick agrees with the point I made in chapter 2, that non-geographical ecclesial communities are also possible, and he says this on the basis of his experience in chaplaincy work:

> My last pastorate was in an "intentional" parish without traditional boundaries. It had a double role. It was a campus-ministry parish which served some 5,000 Catholic college students, faculty and staff, and 500 residential families. We were ready to begin the ACTION community process there, involving both the students and the residential parishioners. So I believe that ACTION communities can be developed within "intentional" or territorial parishes, although some changes would be necessary.

We should also recognize that the geographical principle for base communities, even within a territorial parish, cannot be regarded as the only valid approach. I have presented it as a valuable way of achieving the end of inclusivity. But it is the goal that is important, not the means. There are many churches that sponsor house groups on a less rigid basis, and some of these manage to work on the expectation that all church-members belong to a house group as well as to the larger worshipping community.

The house groups may be dotted around the parish, but which one you join may depend on other factors besides which one is closest. For example, the local group may meet on a Tuesday evening, when you are only free on Wednesdays and Thursdays. Or there may be a daytime group that is more practical for the elderly (who do not like going out at night) or for parents at home with small children (if there is a crèche). Or the youth may like to meet in a group of their own. I see no reason why house groups of this type should not have the potential to grow into basic ecclesial communities in a fuller sense, without needing to go through a geographical reorganization, so long as the sense of universality can find expression through them.

In summary, I suspect that the territorial basis may be the best way of starting a base-community structure. It counts everybody in, it gives odd-bods a sense of belonging somewhere, and it gets across the idea that the basic ecclesial community is not just another group of the kind we have been used to in the first world, but is a fundamentally different conception.

However, base communities have many models and there are no prototypes to be copied. You have to begin with the parish as it is, and not treat it as a blank slate, unless it actually is a new parish. If there is a thriving house-group system already established, you have to work with it, not against it.

Once the fundamental idea of basic ecclesial community has been assimilated, there are no rules about how it should be done – geographically or otherwise. We are all, in the first world, on a journey of discovery, and we can all learn from each other's experience the best ways of getting these communities off the ground. No doubt in the years ahead there will be non-geographical communities to learn from as well as those more like Tony Castle's sections and Richard Ling's ACTION communities.

I said there were two respects in which Dick's communities

differed from the more familiar communities formed in parishes. The other big difference was that he did not form the communities first among regular mass-goers and then expand into mission as a second-stage development, but actually began with evangelization as the first stage of the process. On the other hand "Renew", which is a powerful influence for good and one of the most common forms of community-building within the parish especially in the USA,[5] puts the evangelization phase as the end result of a group's development.

Dick is himself an admirer of "Renew", having promoted it in two different parishes and found "how effectively 'Renew' fosters a renewal of spirit among Catholics and the development of a taste for small group experiences". But he finds that when he has asked small groups of the "Renew" type, "Are your small groups evangelizing?", the constant answer is either "No" or "Not very successfully". Nor is this surprising, for one of the purposes of small groups is to form bonds among the members. "After a group has been together for several meetings, an unspoken truth exists – 'It is not easy for a newcomer to enter this more intimate group.' Of course it is possible. But group members know well, perhaps more in their bones than in their minds, that inclusion of new members poses difficulties."

I believe Dick is right here, and of course it is another reason why the geographical base is so valuable, because it gives people a community to which they can belong by right, without any sense that this is not quite the right group for them, or that they are barging in on someone else's show. Moreover, Dick says, "Catholics who entered our ACTION communities knew from experience that 'Church' meant a gathering of 'evangelized persons'. What is more, having experienced the simplicity of the evangelizing process themselves, they were more motivated and eager to be evangelizers again." Dick reminds us of a point made by the US Jesuit theologian, Avery Dulles, that gives a theological, rather than a psychological, reason for putting evangelizing at the beginning of the process. There is not first something called "being Church" which then looks for "a mission". Rather, there is first "a mission" that requires "a Church".

These, then, were the principal two differences of the ACTION communities over the more intentional groups most parishes were fostering – basing the communities geographically, and evangelizing before forming communities rather than after.

Another criticism that has been made of the ACTION communities is that they were too much "top down": the ground was mapped out and the communities delineated in the parish office in advance of the people's participation. This anxiety about being "top down" rather than "bottom up" is found again and again in the first world, and often stops pastoral agents from initiating anything for fear that it will only be valid if it begins at the grassroots. But the essential point of base communities is to foster a dynamic of "from the bottom up", even though the original initiative and much on-going nurturing has often come from the top down. Dick defends his process against the charge as follows:

1) It is erroneous to believe that the most flourishing of all small Church communities – the base communities of Latin America – or the majority of small Church communities in the US are communities initiated without trained and official leadership.
2) The criticism overlooks the fact that the team was composed of laity.
3) Most significantly, the fundamental issues about small communities are their inclusivity, faithfulness to Gospel values, and dedication to the new creation, not who forms them.

It may be, however, that there is room for developing more flexibility once the communities get under way. Dick's method feels a little like a formula – even it was one that worked brilliantly almost every time it was repeated. The precision of planning sounds programmatic; for example, the fourth meeting always followed a set pattern and Dick always attended it. The overall feel will be thought by many to be very North American – which of course need not be a criticism but a recognition of the distinctive culture of the USA.

It might be a more convincing proof that the local laity really had begun to find their own feet if, for example, communities developed more differences in their pattern of ministries. Once they had grasped the essential point, first that a community needs ministers – ministers who serve the community and ministers who reach out beyond the community – and secondly that everyone has something to offer, then perhaps they might begin to find their own way in how they organize themselves. The really interesting story is the one that begins where Dick's story leaves off: how did the communities proceed once they were left to find their own way?

We always find that building communities takes a lot of work, even here, where the growth was so rapid. Crucial to the whole enterprise was a lot of time spent knocking on doors, and many priests would lack the inclination to do this. But Dick Ling believes that house-to-house visitation is "the one most effective form of active hospitality and evangelization available to us". And he continues, "What better work for a pastor than to get out of his office and meet all of his people, especially those who are hurting the most, to bring them together in ways that they would never be able to do, and to facilitate a genuine sense of what 'Christian' and 'Church' are all about."

This practice of house-to-house visiting is exactly what we saw in the first passage quoted in chapter 4 – from El Salvador – where the priests surprised the people by going out to visit them, house by house, instead of sitting in their office waiting to book in baptisms and funerals. Often something can sound inspiring and romantic when we hear of it happening in a foreign country, which may sound tedious and objectionable if anyone suggests we should try it here at home.

Dick's lasting feelings are a mixture of hope and despondency. He can see that

> . . . small Church communities seriously test the Catholic Church's understanding of power, especially as bishops and popes realize that many small Church communities are being administered by *unordained* women. In a word, small Church communities focus on a very serious *power issue* in Catholicism today, and the Vatican heat seems to be increasing, not cooling down.

This does not of course imply any intention of breaking away and going it alone. "We had no intention of creating wholly autonomous 'little churches' within the parish. Faithful to the long Catholic tradition of small groups that remain united to the larger Church, our ACTION communities saw themselves as integral parts united in the larger 'body' of the parish." It is the idea of being a cell of a larger body once again.

And Dick respects the theological value of hierarchy, even if he wishes it were differently exercised at the moment. "The original sense of 'hierarchy'," he says, is "a 'holy ordering' within the Church, not an ordering from 'top to bottom' but an ordering from the 'centre out'." This idea, and the idea of administration meaning "for the ministers", could not sound more like Leonardo Boff's description of the charism of unity:

> What would the Church be if there were a multiplicity of charisms without any order among them? How would all the members constitute one body, if there were no one to see that the charisms were exercised for the common good? . . . The specific function of the hierarchy (those who are in leadership roles) is not accumulation but integration, making way for unity and harmony among the various services so that any single one does not trip up, drown out, or downplay another . . . . This hierarchical function is carried out by the co-ordinator of a local ecclesial community, by the bishop in his diocese, and by the Pope in the universal Church.[6]

Whatever the disappointments, the glimpse of the dream is irrepressible and so self-evidently good that it goes on feeding hope. Dick writes:

> This is a story of imagination at work, imagination stimulated by the Spirit and the willingness of laity and clergy to listen to the signs of the time . . . . It is a story giving flesh to Jesus' proclamation: "I am the vine, you are the branches". It is a story confirming Paul's vision: "You are the body of Christ". I pray that my enthusiastic if limited skills will add a helpful chapter to this fascinating adventure.

Chapter 7

STARTING FROM THE STREET:
Bombay and Managua

The last three chapters looked at the parish as a starting point. They found that the parish, as an existing, official structure, has great potential as a framework for forming base communities, in a relatively short time, among very many ordinary people, who would not have arrived there by their own efforts or insights. But the parish is not the only possible starting point.

One of the major problems with starting from the parish is that if the parochial clergy are not already converted to the concept of base community, the work cannot begin. And with the conservative restoration that is sweeping through the Catholic Church at the moment, there may be fewer and fewer parish priests with a vision of base community.

There is another way – and that is to begin from another starting point altogether. We can begin to build the new way of being Church, not on the foundations of the old way of being Church, but starting right from scratch. This happens when pastoral agents work with a community "on the street". Instead of working with people who are already church-goers, trying to transform their vision; they work with people who are not church-goers but simply the local community, giving them the Christian vision maybe for the first time.

This is a long process. But it is also a radical one, for there are no presuppositions or established practices to overcome. The Church then is really built from the bottom up.

This chapter and the two following ones look at four attempts at base community, starting from the street. First we look at an article about the Bombay Improvement Trust *chawls* in India, where Paul Vaz began work in the early 1980s. Then we go to Osvaldo

Manzanares *barrio*, Managua, Nicaragua, where the Maryknoll lay missioner, Anne McSweeney, started work among a new *barrio* in 1985.

In the next two chapters I give reports of my visits to British communities in situations of inner-city deprivation. We go to Heath Town, Wolverhampton, where the Hope Community began to operate in 1985. Finally we look at the work of the Anfield Fellowship, Liverpool, initiated by Dave Cave in 1983. These two accounts examine in some depth the issues that arise from work among the poor in the first world, and they form a climax to our exploration throughout the book.

Bombay Improvement Trust chawls

I have chosen this report from Bombay because it presents a method for building basic community in a society which is not predominantly Christian, indeed where only a small minority are Christian. This is increasingly relevant to some parts of the first world, particularly to Europe. The Jesuit, Paul Vaz, tells the story.

> The idea of building basic communities in an urban setting came to me when I was studying theology in Pune. A group of us had opted to do our theology from outside the Jesuit theologate at De Nobili College. We lived in a *chawl* about half a mile away, and using the resources provided by the theologate, attempted to work out an experience-based theology from below. Living outside the seminary, and sharing the life of the people around us, had a profound impact on our theology and on our lives. It was here, being with the people, sharing in their joys and sorrows, their hopes and anxieties,[1] that I began to realize how important communities were, and how it was possible to build communities by gathering people together on issues of common interest, like getting the landlord to supply an electrical connection or to repair a leaking roof.
>
> On coming to Bombay after my seminary studies I was sent to build communities among the urban poor of the city, working out of Seva Niketan, a centre for spiritual and social services run by the Jesuits of the Bombay Province of the Society of Jesus.
>
> After much searching I decided to start work at the BIT (Bombay

Improvement Trust) *chawls*, which lie about a quarter of an hour's walk away to the south of Seva Niketan. The *chawls* are three-storey blocks of one-room tenements, which had been built during the time of the British for the municipal workers of the city. There are twenty blocks in the BIT *chawls*, each with eighty rooms, twenty (ten by fifteen feet) rooms to a floor, with common bathrooms and toilets. A room is normally occupied by a family though there are sometimes more than one, occasionally as many as four families in a single room. In all then there would be about 1,600 families in the *chawls*.

Privacy is obviously an unobtainable luxury here, and the incredible overcrowding has its marked social and psychological consequences. Violent quarrels, high alcoholism, gambling, free consensual marriages are common. The number of children who drop out of school is high. The youth are largely unemployed. They read little, only film magazines, if anything at all. Sports, films, dramas, videos and other escapist entertainments are popular. Feasts like "Ganpati", or "Navatri", "Sai Baba Jayanti", "Diwali", "Buddha Purnima", "Holi" or "Christmas" are high points in the life of the *chawl* and serve to bring the people together.

Religiously, the population of the *chawl* is mixed. Most are Marathi or Gujarati-speaking Hindus. But some 160 families (10 per cent) are Neo-Buddhist *dalits*, about 120 families (8 per cent) are Christian and about 48 families (3 per cent) are Muslim.

How does one go about building communities in such a situation? Initially, I started alone, and after a few months an animating team, which included three professional social workers, was formed. Later we had only two professionals and two voluntary animators. This was strengthened from time to time by young Religious in formation, who joined us for varying periods (from a few months to a year) to gain experience. The team began by creating a rapport with the people in the *chawl*. We celebrated their feasts with them, attended their weddings, talked to them about their needs and expectations. Slowly a rapport was established, needs were expressed, a process of reflection and action began.

Women were the first to respond to such "animation". The Gujarati, Kathiawadi women of Block 4, showed a great desire to learn to read and write, in order to be able to read the numbers of the buses, and the sign-boards in the railway stations. Adult literacy classes were started for them. Soon women from other floors and other blocks joined.

The adult literacy classes brought out the women's needs. As significant words were elicited from the women so that they could be taught to read and write them, it became clear that water was, for the women, a burning issue. Some families had not been getting water for the past four months; others for the past three years! The group decided to take up the issue of water and to do something about it. Various alternatives were suggested and listed. Finally the women realized that since complaints had not worked they would have to go to the Ward Officer to protest. This, of course, required considerable courage on their part, because protesting was not something they had been accustomed to. Both as women and as *dalit* women they had been taught to acquiesce passively in situations, however unjust, never to protest against them. Over a series of meetings, however, their confidence was built up. They were brought to see themselves as human beings like any other, not as members of an oppressed caste and sex. They realized that they had a right to the water and that nothing prevented them from going to the Ward Officer to present their problem to him.

An appointment was made with the Ward Officer and the whole group of women went to meet him in his office. A lively interchange followed. The somewhat sarcastic questions of the Officer, who obviously believed that *dalit* women should know their place ("Why do you need water?"; "I know why you are not getting enough water, because you bathe twice daily: see how well you are dressed today") were met with replies that were admirably clear, straightforward and honest. A memorandum carrying the signatures of sixty families was handed to the Ward Officer, and he agreed to come to the *chawls* next day to verify the problem for himself.

Next day, he did turn up as promised and visited the first and second floors of the block. The task of taking him around and showing him the taps and the connections was entrusted to the women of each floor. On his return he ordered the water connection to be laid.

I have narrated this incident at some length because, insignificant as it seems, it was a crucial point in the process of community-building in the BIT *chawls*, and offers a good illustration of the dynamics of community animation. Talking to the people elicits an immediate need (literacy). Responding to this need leads to the awareness of a more basic need (water). Organizing the people to tackle this as a group, leads to awareness of themselves as a community. For not only was the people's self-image greatly boosted by the success of their agitation, but they began to reflect on the reasons for their success. These reasons were analysed at their next meeting, and were formulated by them as follows: We succeeded because 1) we were all united and supported each other; 2) we spoke up boldly and expressed our problem openly; and 3) we realized that we have a right to water as much as any other human being. These three points became the refrain for every subsequent meeting, reminding the women that in common action lay their strength.

The process of awareness-building grew spontaneously. News of what had happened reached other blocks, and groups of women from the other blocks too began to get together to discuss their problems and do something about them. Issues like rations, drainage, sanitation were taken up. Gradually, interest shifted to deeper, cultural issues like those of the rejection of girl-children in Indian society, the incidence of rape, wife-beating, the problem of the dowry system, and so on.

At the same time an animator of our team began to work with the youth of the area. Contact was established with some of the youth who used to meet from time to time in tea shops. Film appreciation, play-acting, picnics, and training camps were used to bring them together. Somewhat prematurely (because I had to go for my Tertianship, the last stage in my Jesuit formation) the youth were organized into a group, which they called the Organization for a Better Society. Committees were appointed to take care of the following issues: 1) religious affairs; 2) children's activities; 3) supportive education; and 4) a study circle.

Each committee had its own area of work. Where there was a concentration of Christians, the religious affairs committee tried to organize meaningful eucharists for them, arranged for their faith formation through seasonal celebrations like those of Advent and Lent, and organized floor feasts. For this they used a variety of methods; like drama, puppetry, street exhibitions, posters, flash cards and group discussion; often with considerable creativity.

Seeing the Christians celebrate their feasts in meaningful ways, the Hindus thought, "Why not we?" So for "Hanuman Jayanti" they put up a thought-provoking drama showing the *hanumans* of today, the little *dadas* pushing people around in the ration queues, or the big bully-boy who does not attend school but forcibly takes away the notes of his little companion. They lord it over others, until the real Lord Hanuman comes along and says: "I was the Lord of the universe, the protector of the weak and oppressed, see what you have made me today!"

Community-building in the BIT *chawls* has proved to be a creative and challenging task. It is by no means easy to animate people forced for decades to a passive acceptance of their *karma*, brainwashed by religion and society into a deep sense of their inadequacy and helplessness. Animators, too, are hard to find, because their work is taxing and their salaries low. Building up communities inevitably leads to involvement in issues which are full of risks, and to forms of action that are full of uncertainty. There are no precedents, no clear-cut guidelines in this work. "Wayfarer, there is no way," as the poet has said, "you make your way by walking."

And yet, in spite of all this, the work is immensely satisfying and productive. There are few things more stirring than to see a group of oppressed people come alive, build up their confidence in themselves, break their "culture of silence" and stand up in public to tell their story, and find solidarity in the struggle for their rights.[2]

Reflection

The work in Bombay is of relevance to those first-world contexts where many people have no religion at all, or where a sizeable and growing minority are Muslims (as in Britain). The method used is, in essence, the same as that used for basic communities in Catholic countries, but the Christian element plays a more limited role in the total community project.

However it is important to notice that it does have a place: whether in a multi-religious community, or in a secular society, there are times when it is appropriate for Christians to meet together on their own for worship, even if the social projects are organized on a non-religious basis. In those first-world countries where Christians are a minority group, it may be appropriate for the bulk of community work among the poor to be secular in its nature; but that is not to deny that a basic Christian community has a role in the midst of the wider community.

The basic method of work – to meet people on their own ground and listen to their needs before attempting to plan anything for them – is as applicable to the first world as it is to Bombay. It is an approach that we see well exemplified in the next example, from a *barrio* in Managua, where there is not yet a basic ecclesial community but where a preliminary process has begun that might eventually flower into that.

Osvaldo Manzanares barrio, *Managua*

I met the US lay missioner, Anne McSweeney, at her house in a poor barrio of Managua called Osvaldo Manzanares, in January 1989. She gave me a simple but delicious lunch, over which we talked, and then she walked me through the *barrio*, where I was asked a blurry question by a wandering drunk. "Ignore him," said Anne, "he's asking you if you're a virgin."

She introduced me to her neighbours: the husband, who had lost a leg in the insurrection, said how honoured he was that I should have come halfway round the world to visit people like them. When I asked if I could have a photo taken of me with the family, I was able to count twelve happy, smiling children who clustered in for it.

Anne came to Nicaragua with Maryknoll, in July 1985, on a three-year contract. They prefer to use the term "missioner", to get away from the old associations of "missionary". "Missionaries were people who made women wear bras," one of Anne's colleagues explained to me. Anne's previous experience had been in neighbourhood and tenant organizing, and she had also worked for a diocese doing parish social ministry. With Maryknoll she did a four-month orientation course and four months of language school before she was sent to Managua. Her method of working reflects the principles of Maryknoll missioners wherever they are found.

One of Maryknoll's priorities at that date was to work in the new *barrios*, because the kind of pastoral attention provided by parishes usually does not filter down to them. It was November by the time Anne knew which *barrio* she was going to move into, along with two other missioners, after spending weeks "bouncing around from office to office", getting lists of new neighbourhoods and investigating the possibilities of each. They wanted to have some sort of entrance into the neighbourhood, and they were looking for somewhere where there was room for the work to grow into surrounding squatter settlements. "We also did not want to come into direct conflict with the archdiocese, so we were looking for a place where we could move in and not have a conflictual situation with the pastor. Here the community organization very much welcomed us in, so it fitted all of our criteria."

The *barrio* of Osvaldo Manzanares is a resettlement area, started in 1983, for people who were moved from the lake shore because of flooding. These form nearly half the population of the *barrio*, with the remainder coming to the capital from the country, either because of the Contra war and its destructive effects on agriculture, or because of the general trend all over the third world towards urbanization. "They might move into a very, very simple house," Anne told me. "Some of them are just cardboard and plastic when they first move in."

It was February 1986 by the time Anne and her colleagues were able to move into the simple wooden house, which they had built for them. It looks like a primitive shack from the outside, but inside it is attractively rustic, with a dirt floor and a couple of typical Nicaraguan rocking chairs, nailed together from boards. Bookcases and beds were covered in plastic sheeting because of the dust. "Imagine designing a house for Nicaragua when you've been here for just a couple of months," Anne said. "We made a few mistakes. We should have put the door over there so we could have caught the rain coming off the roof, because we have to go down the street for water."

The house is a little larger than most in the *barrio*, simply because it has three bedrooms. "We decided that we had needs that needed taking care of or we would go nuts, so we had separate rooms."

They also had a septic tank connected to the sink "for hygiene", which only a few others in the neighbourhood have. But they decided to stick with a dirt floor, though "it turns out the two are very connected: what people do with their waste water is throw it on the floor to keep the dust down. I end up having to catch my water before it goes down the drain so I can throw it." In the yard outside is a latrine in a little shed – just a very deep hole with a cement seat on top. "I suppose they must fill up at some point but I'm not even coming close on this one." The smell is rather less than that of the pig next door, which "is the noisiest pig in the neighbourhood, maybe in the country".

"When we got here we decided we did not really want to come in with our own agenda, so we spent longer than I ever thought possible visiting people and not doing anything very programmatic, so we could get a sense of what people's needs were. And I think that served us well, though it was very hard to do, not to dig right in. The thing that came through strongest was the need to do something with youth, because you've probably noticed that over 50 per cent of Nicaragua is under fifteen years old, and I think in this *barrio* it is a lot higher than that." There was "just a real need to give them something to do."

Anne and her colleagues began by asking the co-ordinators of each block for the names of a couple of kids who were bright at school – two kids from each block was the aim. In that way they tried to select the most talented youth to work with, so the work would have the maximum impact, and also so as to get a fairer distribution around the neighbourhood rather than concentrating on those they knew best because they lived closest. By December they were running a course on leadership skills for the under-fifteens, teaching them how to animate a group and run a project, "emphasizing the need to plan it, to do it and evaluate".

She feels leadership skills are much needed because "although Nicaragua has had its revolution, a lot of people at the base are still not comfortable with any other kinds of leadership models than what they had known for years and years." So they organized "a weekly meeting where we do exercises in co-operation and leadership, and teach them how to run meetings and that kind of thing. And they have a weekly practical where they run a recreation programme for younger children, which has worked out pretty well. It's mostly baseball, but not always." While we were speaking, children wandered up to the open door to have a look and say "*hola!*"; one boy looked through the window and talked to Anne about the volley-ball game the youth group was organizing that weekend.

"Because they are a pretty well organized group, at one point the woman in charge of health for the neighbourhood came to us and asked if the youth could help with the vaccination campaign; and they actually ended up running it, doing everything except giving the injections. They got a much higher rate of vaccination than ever before, principally because they had so much energy; and they went around in groups, advertising it, making up their own little jingles. It was a lot of fun. There are always a few problems, so afterwards we did an evaluation and they made copies of it for the health centre and for the woman who was in charge of health. She now has a lot more respect for them. Some of the things that went wrong were her responsibility, and they did not go wrong the next time."

After that they joined in the national campaign "For the Defence of the Children", which is largely aimed at reducing the incidence of diarrhoea. The kids worked at filling in holes so the fly and mosquito population went down, and they wrote some very simple stories on big placards which they took to corners of the *barrio* and read to children and their parents: like "Miguel is playing baseball and he falls down and scrapes his knee, and this is how his friends help him clean it up", or "Carlito gets malaria" which "takes you through how he gets malaria – because he has got all these places where mosquitoes collect in his house."

"They have written all these stories and illustrated them themselves. The adults sometimes gather round too, to hear the stories, which I think is also having a good effect." All this is organized by children between ten and fourteen in age – it may sound young but "some of the leaders of the neighbourhood groups are sixteen or seventeen, so we figured you work with the younger kids and eventually it is going to spill over".

After a few years the other two missioners went on to other work elsewhere, and I asked Anne how she felt about living alone now in the house: "Personally, socially, I am not much into living alone, but I did not think I would feel frightened. Then the first week that Paddy left I was having all these nightmares, and I realized, when I started thinking about it, that it had a little bit of basis in fact. "*O la Patricia se fue, está solita, povrecita* – Paddy's gone, you're alone, you poor thing." The two-year-olds were saying it to me, the ninety-year-olds were saying it to me, which meant that everybody knew that I was alone. I think there are some good reasons to maybe take some precautions and just be pretty careful. I lock the door at night, for sure. But I feel pretty secure in the neighbourhood: my neighbours are very good and they watch out for me in a lot of different ways."

One of Anne's plans is to investigate the possibility of a girls' group, "because the boys are too wild and there are not many girls in the youth group – four out of twenty. I know there are girls who are interested in it." There are several options for what that group might do. "One would be to do the same kind of things – leadership training. Another possibility would be to do some kind of conscientization about what it is to be a woman in Nicaragua today, and there are some good resources on that that we could look at. People tell you with great pride that here women are liberated. It's all relative. Nicaragua is still a tremendously *machista* society in a lot of ways, in terms of attitudes, but the structures are there for women to be very liberated. But since the interest is coming from them I might open it up to them at the first meeting to see if they have ideas."

I asked Anne, "Is this a base community here?" "No," she said. "We have a reflection group that is moving towards becoming a base community but it's really not at that point yet." She explained that this biblical reflection group started "by people realizing that we were missioners and asking us for something like that. Really we started with one woman who asked us to do something and she began inviting other people in." It averages about ten people, "though people come in and out. There is one man who is slightly retarded in the group, and the group are all good with him for that. And there are people who are super-intelligent, too. So it's a good mix, and there's men and women, and some of them are older and some are younger."

They meet for a couple of hours one evening a week, beginning with a minute or so to collect themselves in silence. Then each one shares something of what has been going on in the last week "in the family, in their personal lives, in the neighbourhood, in the country, and occasionally we hit the world scene, but not too often". That takes about an hour, after which they read the gospel for the coming Sunday, and try to relate the two. "Most people in the group are not really comfortable with reading aloud, but they will all do it at one point or another."

"After we read we would do a summary, in our own words, of what had happened, just to make sure everyone has understood it. That has been something for people to really discipline themselves on – not to start reflecting before it is clear that everybody has understood what has gone on. But they have got pretty good at that; and we rotate the facilitation of the group among the members, so they have all had to be in the role of putting a stop on someone who plunges into reflection; so that has helped each one of them to stop doing it, too. And then we do a reflection on how it relates to what was just talked about, or if it relates to something that was not talked about at the beginning."

At the end they sing, and the children come and join in that, which makes it *más alegre* – more lively. (*Alegría* – liveliness, fun, enjoyment – is a key element in Latin American base communities.) On the whole people are not much inhibited about singing. "Living around here you hear people singing all the time. To do that you have to either not care or have a lot of confidence, because clearly everybody else can hear you; I mean we are just living too close not to hear."

Most people are Catholics, though "there are a number of evangelical sects that operate in the *barrio* in one way or another. They fill a need – to meet and sing and clap hands. There are a few of them that are pretty anti-Catholic." Most people "don't even come close to what we would call practising Catholic. They are mostly baptized. They would not usually go to the nearest parish for baptism. Most of them, if they have lived in Managua before, would go to where they had lived before. Or a lot of folks work around the oriental market and there is a church there, so they go there. Then there is a whole group of people who have found out where you have to go to the least amount of talks about baptism, like people the world over.

"So people do baptize their children, but they do not mostly go to mass. Maybe 3 per cent or 4 per cent of the people would go to mass, although people would participate in popular religiosity. The *Purísima*, the feast of the Immaculate Conception, is a big deal; and lots of people in this neighbourhood would have altars in their houses for that. But most people would not relate to a parish at all. There is a parish that does cover us territorially, but it does not have anything to do with this neighbourhood. What is kind of neat about the reflection group is that it does give people a chance, another way of participating in Church life, in spiritual life."

At what point would the Bible reflection group qualify as a proper basic ecclesial community? "When they start looking beyond themselves. They do that individually, and at times they have done things like visiting sick members, but always members of the group. When they start really as a group having the deeds that follow their faith, doing projects in the locality, then I would call them a Christian community."

When might that happen? The reflection group had started about a year and a half ago, so Anne felt the next stage "may happen soon", but "it's probably going to take me doing a bit of pushing in that direction." Another step in the process would be to "plug into the national stuff that is going on", through the CNP (*Comisión Nacional Permanente*), which co-ordinates the basic ecclesial communities in the country. "It is important to do that in terms of a wider perspective."

Reflection

My visit to Anne made a lasting impression on me, not only for her own gentle and sympathetic personality, but for the eminent sense and clarity of the way she worked. On the one hand, she was responding quite specifically to one particular cultural situation in one particular place. But on the other, the general approach – listening, befriending, responding, planning, acting and evaluating – was of universal applicability, and I was stunned by its obviousness and simplicity. "This can be done anywhere," I thought. And more than that: "This should be done everywhere."

Chapter 8

STARTING FROM THE STREET:

The Hope Community

Heath Town is an estate of multiple deprivation, built in the late sixties in Wolverhampton, an industrial town in the Midlands of England. It consists of nine tall tower blocks and other lower blocks of maisonettes, housing 3–4,000 people. One of the local residents wrote in a poem:

> I sometimes through my windows stare
> And see but concrete everywhere . . .
> It might have worked if thought had gone
> Into the things that would go wrong.[1]

The estate has a reputation for drug dealing, racial tensions, prostitution, vandalism and all the other problems associated with rough estates. Many of the flats are unoccupied, despite the overall housing problem, as people are afraid to move into such an area. Over 80 per cent of the residents are on social benefit, and unemployment is extremely high, though there are many low-paid jobs on offer to the unemployed at the local "Project Shop". Among the graffiti that I found on the stairs were "Gas all blacks", "Death to nigger-lovers" and "Do not mess with white man". During a police raid for drugs in May 1989, with full riot shields, searchlights and helicopters, it was said that crack was found.

Sister Margaret Walsh told me the story of how the Hope Community came to be founded on the estate. Her congregation, the Sisters of the Infant Jesus, was founded in the seventeenth century for women to go to people "in their surrounddings", "without making vows or being cloistered". After nine years of teaching she had begun to feel she would like a move in the direction of that original charism, which she describes as "working alongside the little ones". She wanted to be "more radically involved" and to work in the inner city.

In 1985 she was granted the freedom from her congregation to go and explore. When she arrived in the town – where the congregation already had a house – a local parish priest came to see her and asked if she would be interested in helping in his parish, particularly with the hospital chaplaincy work. He drove her over to his presbytery, and on the way they passed through the estate. Immediately Margaret began to feel a tug, and that first sight of the estate remained vividly in her memory. The priest was talking about the hospital, and she kept on wanting to ask, "But what about this estate?" It was clear that he did not have the time to do much pastoral work on the estate, although it was within his parish boundary. Margaret agreed to go and help at the hospital, but she asked at the same time, "Can we just do some census work down the road as well?"

Meeting the people

And so Margaret and two other Infant Jesus sisters began work at Heath Town in January 1985. Margaret and another sister went as a pair, while the third, "who was big and brave", went by herself. They just took the lift to the top floor and knocked all the way down. In any block, she explained, "You are lucky if three people will answer the door. So of course we were soon at the bottom."

But a few did open. The sisters were absolutely delighted because they had knocked at so many. They just said they were from St Patrick's parish, coming to say hello to people. Some people then welcomed them in, and they began to hear stories of isolation and fear, of loneliness and despair. Originally they took the names and addresses of the Catholics, but very early on they found the focus moved from the census to simply listening to people's stories.

Two of the sisters did the visiting full time, though Margaret was still dividing her work between the estate and the hospital. But they all found it was difficult to leave in the evenings and return to the different world of their religious house. And so in October 1985 they moved into the estate to live, taking a couple of the unoccupied maisonettes. By the time they moved in they knew a lot of people, many of whom are still among their most faithful visitors, and these new friends were there to welcome them when they moved in.

Moving in was a tremendous advantage, said Margaret. "We can talk about 'we' and 'us' instead of 'you'. It makes such a difference." And she gave as an example the experience of going to the laundry-room at the bottom of the block, and returning with all your washing, and finding the lift has broken down. If you live there, then you really know what the difficulties are.

There were plenty of warning voices over their move. Some friends wondered if they could possibly fit in or be accepted, when they were so different from anyone else on the estate in terms of background and professional training. Margaret points out that there was another big difference: they chose to move in, but few others on the estate were there by choice. They were also warned of the dangers of being mugged or having their flat broken into. But five years later they are able to say that they have experienced very little violence, hostility or theft, even though they keep open house. Their neighbours are ready to accompany and protect them if there is any problem or if it is late at night. But during one of my visits Margaret and I crossed the estate after dark without a second thought about a chaperon: Margaret explained she was well-known so that there was no danger at all.

Within a year the Community began to include laity and members of other churches, both men and women, and there has been quite a turnover of personnel over the years. Margaret is convinced that in the British context the Gospel can only be communicated convincingly when there is an interdenominational approach. As the Community took in those who were not Infant Jesus sisters, it also took on the name "the Hope Community", as a reminder of the need to stand ready to explain the hope that was in them (1 Peter 3:15) in the face of so much depression around.

Margaret describes the Hope Community as "a series of concentric circles. The central nucleus are those of us who belong to the Sisters of the Infant Jesus. The inner circle are those who have committed themselves to living with us for various lengths of time. And there are outer circles of neighbours and friends, who are involved with us in many different ways."[2] If Margaret was pleased to be able to say "we" about membership of the estate, so in the same way the local regulars happily say "we" about membership of the Hope

Community. "*We* have a chapel next door," said one local woman during my visit. Another local who was picked up by the police asked them to put a call through to the mother superior of his Community – meaning Margaret Walsh.

From the beginning the policy was to look for opportunities to gather people together, in whatever way seemed natural. One day, shortly after the initial move, Margaret and her colleagues were invited to a Tupperware party. At the end they suggested that the group should not go home without arranging another get-together. No one else was offering, so the Hope Community took the opportunity to invite everyone to tea at their place, and that was the beginning of their open house facility.

The flat-to-flat visiting, of course, continued after the move in, and as time went on they became an established presence, with many more reasons to knock on doors. From all their contacts the Community have constructed visiting lists, and the word has got around so that they now find more people know them than they know. At Christmas and Easter time they visit every home in the estate with seasonal greetings.

Sometimes they ask one resident from a block to take them to visit all their friends – a process which can take weeks. Or there may be visiting work connected with the local housing or social services departments. Recently there was a new census done on housing, in collaboration with the housing authority, and when an estate management committee was being set up, that too provided an occasion for visiting new people and asking if they would be interested. Opportunities like this, says Margaret, give you a great chance to go into people's homes with your questions and really listen to them.

Often a reason for visiting is that someone new is known to have moved in, and sometimes these people arrive with nothing other than their key – not so much as a mattress or a table or chair. On one of my visits I met a girl who had just arrived, fleeing from another estate where she was being threatened by her boyfriend's former girlfriend. She came to Heath Town with her two toddlers, the clothes they stood up in, the television and the video – nothing more. The Hope Community kitted her out with towels, bedding and some basic kitchen equipment from a store that is kept available for such emergencies.

Economic problems

Poverty on the estate is intense: it is the only area I know of that has a cut-price bread shop, for loaves that are a day old. A lot of second-hand buying and selling goes on between residents, as people find themselves literally penniless and hungry and look around for something that they can sell.

Margaret explained there were two causes of the poverty. Firstly the benefits are pitifully low, especially for young single parents (which is the condition of many on the estate; in fact, another member of the Hope Community told me she could only think of about two stable families). People only end up being housed in Heath Town, Margaret explained, when they are in desperate social circumstances, and then on top of their personal woes they may find they have no cooker. "You get fed up living on sandwiches and cold drinks. Where are they going to get £150–200 for a cooker? People wait months around here for a cooker. A kettle is cheaper, they might have some chance of getting that within a few weeks."

The other cause is that many people cannot budget. Money goes on drink and drugs, on betting and cigarettes. I went into the Department of Social Security with a member of the Hope Community and spoke to a woman there who was applying for some emergency cash, as she had nothing to feed her children on over the weekend. She explained to us that she could not make ends meet on the benefit she got, taking into account her hire-purchase commitments and also a satellite dish. I noticed there were a lot of satellite dishes mushrooming out from the walls of the blocks. They make a strange complement to the graffiti-infested walls.

"I can understand it perfectly," Margaret said, of the financial mismanagement. "They get very depressed, and then at last there is some hope in the week, and the temptation is to have a good time at least that once. Eat, drink and be merry and tomorrow we die." She told me of one of their regulars, who goes hungry for at least two days every week: when he gets his benefit he spends it straight-away that night on fruit machines. For many years he was insti-tutionalized, and "if he was still in an institution someone would be helping him to budget. I'm not saying he should be, by the way, but the reality is that he needs somebody: it will take him ages to grasp that he needs two boxes of cornflakes a week and not just one." One of the evenings I was with the Community, Margaret gave out money twice: "People were desperate and they had no food." She insists the loans are paid back, which they always are, although sometimes she has to remind them. "If you are a soft touch you are not helping them."

At one time they ran a regular open house for most of the day, just turning people out at meal times, so at least they could eat in peace. But when the New Start Day Centre opened on the estate – which is primarily for those with mental health problems but also has an open house facility – the Community liaised with them so as not to duplicate resources. Now the Hope Community is open only when New Start is closed, and New Start uses the Hope Com-munity's pool table on Tuesday mornings.

One limitation of the open house policy had been that the same faces turned up again and again, though most days there was some-one new as well. The regulars would arrive first around eleven, come back after lunch at half past two, and again around half past seven after the evening meal. Some of these people have no electricity at home because of unpaid bills, so they are able to find some warmth and a cup of tea at the Hope Community. But the constant flow of visitors can be wearing for the resident members, and they do not always have enough personnel to staff the house during the day. They place a priority on being out and about.

Organized events

Every Friday the resident members of the Hope Community meet together with another sister, who does not live on the estate but comes to visit several days a week, and sometimes the local priest comes too. They share how the visiting has gone that week, and talk about issues on the estate. Then once a month they meet together with the staff of all the local churches for prayer and tea and a good chat – there are two Anglican churches and a black Pentecostal church, as well as the Catholic parish. Recently this ecumenical team employed two community workers – one black and one white. One of the Anglican clergy did the fund-raising for the job, but all the churches are represented on the management committee. There are links also with the Good Shepherd Brothers, who have a house in the centre of the town: they sometimes provide food or clothing. And Margaret is now on the management of the "Breach" project, which takes some of its inspiration from the "Alinsky" method of community organizing.

The Community runs some programmed events, though of a very informal and flexible nature. On Thursday evenings they have a meeting on building community together, which is a discussion on human values, for example, "What makes a flat a home?" Some of those who come are not Christians, and they remind the group not to let the discussion become too religious but to include everybody. Part of the meeting time goes to local news, and part to third-world issues, so that the problems of the estate are seen in a broader context. Third-world issues "always give rise to lively discussion and real concern for brothers and sisters in greater need",[3] says Margaret. And there has been great excitement over writing to prisoners of conscience, taking action to save trees or signing petitions to banks.

Videos are shown one evening a week – while I was there they were in the middle of Zeffirelli's *Jesus of Nazareth*. And once a week they celebrate birthdays with a cake: in the hallway is a calendar and people are invited to write in their date. If they do not turn up they still get a slice of cake brought round afterwards. There have also been day trips organized and even weekends away. "The opportunity to leave the concrete and some of the pressures of life here, is so re-creating! During much of the time we laugh and talk and sing, but quite a lot of it is spent in silent wonder at the beauty and extravagance of God's creation. It is really great to watch the faces of the children when they see wide open spaces. As soon as they get out of the coach they usually begin to run and run until they are exhausted!"[4]

Another regular spot is the "shared table", where one of the local residents offers the use of their flat, and people come bringing food to share, Bibles and hymn-books. Members of the Hope Community often go along in the days beforehand to help the host prepare the flat: sometimes they need chairs and mugs brought round for the guests, and sometimes they need help in a major clean-up. A sense of dignity can grow in a person as they find themselves then able to offer hospitality in a neat and clean flat, where others can come and enjoy themselves. I was told by a black youth, "People just don't realize how much it meant to me and my mum to have the shared table in our home."

There is also an invitation to join the Community at prayer. In all the years the Community have been there no one has yet joined them for Morning Prayer, at 7.30 a.m. "They know it is on, but eleven or twelve o'clock is a more normal time for them to be up and about." But Night Prayer, at 9.30 p.m., is often a wider community event. People will be sitting around smoking and drinking tea, and the invitation will be offered, "We're going to Prayer now. Do you want to join us?" leaving people to feel entirely free either way. The Morning Prayer is based on the Office, but Night Prayer is much more flexible, depending on who is there and what the needs are, and over the years the participation of local people has grown a lot. Margaret remembers one evening particularly vividly:

"We do a lot about community and unity and togetherness, about forgiveness and reconciliation – all of those kind of topics. One evening we began talking about some situation of hopelessness, and from that we went on to talk about darkness and light, then forgiveness, then the difficulty we have in forgiving ourselves or even admitting we are in darkness. Then somebody said, 'It is a real big help to actually tell somebody else,' and then he went on, talking about situations in his own life when he did very naughty things . . . . He said he had done that, but he told somebody and it broke the darkness for him. And that released a whole lot of stories: 'I remember once . . .' There was tremendous release in the group. We went then from there to the chapel (as on Tuesday nights we have shared prayer) and I used the Miserere and some of the Psalms, and the whole thing continued into prayer. It was beautiful. You have to be so flexible, because you do not know if these things will happen or not, and if they do, they do. You adapt your programme then to suit, if you can."

Prayer can happen spontaneously, at any time of day or night. Margaret tells of an incident one evening, which illustrated the people's "deep, childlike trust in a God who cares and who is in everything. A neighbour called late one night, wanting to talk about her son in prison. After listening to her, and praying together for a while, I turned to give her my full attention when I heard her say, 'And now I want to talk to you, because you are a mother like me and you understand how a son can break a mother's heart.' I quickly realized that it was Mary, the mother of God, with whom she wanted to speak."[5]

On Tuesday evenings there is a discussion of local issues in the light of the scriptures. Talking about the Bible began easily and very simply, explained Margaret. When a member of the Hope Community went out to visit people it might seem natural on occasions to say, "Would you like us to pray with you?", and sometimes the person would show them proudly that they had a Bible. Then Margaret might ask, "What is your favourite Bible story?" and maybe read it to them. "So from that we detected a lot of interest in the scriptures at an early stage. Then we said, let's offer something on it." The Tuesday sessions begin with local social issues, and then go on to ask, "What does God say? What does the Bible say?".

At one time there was also a Bible study session, which rather than beginning with the local reality, gave instruction on the structure of the scriptures and where they came from. So there have been the two approaches: the contextual approach and the straight teaching;

and Margaret Walsh recognizes the need for both. But the second group was dropped because of lack of staff. "There is a great hunger for it, a great need, and great appreciation when it happened, but we just have not got the personnel."

Scripture reflection is at 7.30 p.m., but I noticed that people do not turn up at that time specially for it. That is not the way things happen in Heath Town. "It is difficult for them to slot into a time-table of meetings when, for many, the only appointment they have to keep is their fortnightly signing on, at the Department of Social Security, and this is a negative experience they would prefer to forget!"[6] And so "you just get used to the fact that people do not have the same idea of time as we have. Some can't read the clock and so they come here and say 'Is it time yet?' . . . 'Is it time yet?' . . . 'Is it time yet?' . . ." Sometimes Margaret will say, rather than "Another half hour", "You will have time for two more cups of tea and then you can come back."

On my visit, half of those who were sitting around accepted the invitation to come next door for scripture reflection. We began with a hymn from the Community's own hymn-book, led on the guitar. Some could read and some could not. Then a lively discussion about Jesus started in a very easy manner. There was no problem about getting people talking, though there could be more problems about keeping to the point. "You know when you start something," explains Margaret, "that there will be several interruptions during it and you will have to go back to the beginning again. But that reinforces what you are doing."

Last but by no means least are the Celebrations, that are arranged every six weeks in the local community centre. These are Christian liturgies, devised and executed by the people, after weeks of preparation. "The scene often looks a bit chaotic to newcomers, especially visitors, who are more used to orderly church services," Margaret warns. "Young children wander freely about, cigarettes are sometimes passed round, the occasional dog seeks admittance."[7] But this is true liturgy, created from the bottom up. "It is interesting to note how many elements of the Church's liturgy have emerged since we began our local liturgy," Margaret notices. I attended one in November 1990, on the theme of Building Bridges.

Building Bridges

Chairs were arranged in a large semi-circle, with three or four rows (there were about a hundred people there by the end), and we faced a wall with a large star symbol pegged out in multi-coloured wool. There was also a little table with a big candle and a few other bits and pieces.

The first announcement is about fire exits and extinguishers, given by a local man who has just been given a second-hand suit by the Good Shepherd brothers, and who feels a new burst of confidence because he knows he looks smart. Then we are straight into the first song, with music provided on this occasion by the New Creation community guitar group, who have come from Liverpool, and words flashed up on the wall by an overhead projector.

Now another man, with a bad limp, comes forward to say in a loud, clear voice "Good afternoon, ladies and gentlemen. You are all very welcome," before sitting down again hurriedly and happily with his task complete. A stout lady now invites us all to "find someone you have not met before and tell them your name". A happy buzz fills the room, as the opening greeting of our liturgy gets well under way. The introductions conclude with the lighting of the candle: "This is a symbol of Christ, ladies and gentlemen."

Now a young black guy, who is evidently intelligent but today is looking nervous, steps forward to announce: "The theme of this Celebration is Building Bridges of unity and love. In order to do this, we know that we must be ready to forgive ourselves and others . . . . If you would all like to close your eyes, I will read what Martin Luther King had to say; then we can remain in silence for a little while, and make his dream our own."

> I have a dream today . . .
> All of God's children,
> Black men and white men,
> Jews and Gentiles,
> Protestants and Catholics,
> Will be able to join hands and sing
> In the words of the black people's old song,
> Free at last, free at last,

Thank God almighty,
We are free at last.

After a silence we sing, "When I needed a neighbour were you there?" This concludes what we could perhaps recognize as the penitential rite.

It is followed by a dramatic sketch, performed by two girls, one of whom lives on the estate. One girl comes into the laundry and mimes putting her washing in the machine, pouring in the powder, and turning it on. No sooner has it started than another enters, with her washing. "What are doing with your washing in the machine?" she demands. "This is supposed to be my wash-time."

"Well no one was using it, so I thought it was free," says the first.

The other storms at her, "I always use it at this time. I have to go out in an hour and how can I do my washing then?" and so the slanging match gets under way. Eventually the first girl apologizes and offers to put the other girl's washing through the machine for her. She in turn is grateful and offers a cup of tea. All ends in friendship and peace, with declarations of mutual gratitude.

Now a local, unemployed man goes to the table and produces a basket with plaited strands of rainbow-coloured wool. He speaks quietly (some had to strain to hear) but with such conviction that it was riveting to listen to:

We are all brothers and sisters. That is true even if we do not know each other. But the thing about a bridge is this: it is narrow, and so we meet the person coming towards us. If we will only let ourselves do that, then we will really come to know each other as brother and sister.

God has a bridge: it is the rainbow. The colours of the rainbow remind us how rich and varied God's creation is. We make up a rainbow of life, here at Heath Town. And at the end of the rainbow there is a treasure. That treasure is love.

If we were born in hospital, a band was placed on our wrist, so that everyone knew who we were. That way there were no risks or chances when it came to caring for us. Today we invite you to wear a wrist band, bearing the colours of the rainbow. So we are sending round the children. They will give you a band plaited from wool to tie onto your neighbour's wrist.

You cannot tie a strand of wool with one hand, so co-operation between neighbours – between brothers and sisters – is essential for this exercise, and I wear my rainbow-coloured wrist-band for days afterwards, with pride.

Now a plump but pretty blond girl (who has been rushing out to the loo every five minutes, out of nerves) sings in her lovely voice "I'd like to teach the world to sing". Next comes a testimony. Margaret "interviews" a local woman who has had a serious fire in her home, when the electric blanket on her bed caught fire. The interview technique helps her to make all the points that she planned on saying in a careful preparation for this moment, and to say them freshly, without needing to read any notes.

"In spite of my tremendous fear and panic, I was aware of the many people who had gathered outside trying to help. I could see the horror and frustration on their faces, and some were actually screaming." But in hospital, in considerable pain from burns, "I was overwhelmed by the flowers, letters and cards I received. I believe that the support I received gave me the strength to carry on." A collection was organized and "people were very generous and gave gladly, even though only a few actually knew me. When I came home to my new flat I was overwhelmed by the love and care that had gone into preparing it – several people including the sisters worked almost round the clock so that it would be ready in time." But lying in hospital was a time of a new and unexpected experience, "that's very difficult for me to describe. I really felt closer to the Lord than I'd ever felt before, and in spite of being ill and in a great deal of distress, I felt deep inside a sense of peace, and knew because of this that everything would be OK even if I died."

When she finishes this testimony a man from a local parish congregation leads some prayers. He invites us to think what we would like to give thanks for, and then say it aloud if we wish. The response is ready: thanks are given for "peace of mind", for "children and babies", for "the New Start Day Centre". Now he invites us to think who we would like to pray for. Someone mentions his sister who has been ill for twenty-four years. Someone else brings our attention to a local girl who has just been killed in a road accident, and whose parents are with us that day. (Around this point of the celebration there is some muttering near the door from some people who have wandered in and think the whole thing "a load of crap".)

The prayers are followed by a poem read by a young woman in a red and black jersey trouser-suit, who wrote it herself:

> In Heath Town lies,
> Amongst its spies,
> The Hope Community,
> Freedom and unity . . . .
>
> Freedom for people, from the stress,
> Freedom from burdens, and life's mess,
> Freedom to love, to bring peace, and hope,
> That with God's help we all will cope.
>
> It's not easy being unemployed,
> Some people cope, some get annoyed,
> But with God's help we're overjoyed . . .
>
> Amongst the concrete blocks so high
> Look above and see the birds fly.
> There lies a dawning, in the sky.[8]

After a sung "Our Father", in echo mode, we came to the next symbolic act. From the table are produced pieces of card, which have been cut out by the local people in the shape of bridges, coloured in rainbow colours on one side and bearing a text from the Bible hand-written on the other. We each draw one out of the baskets carried around by the children, and are invited to read aloud our text if we wish. Some who cannot read get their neighbour to read it for them. And so, from around the room, come the words of scripture, each text read by someone who likes it enough to want to share it with the rest of us. Words of comfort and encouragement flow around us: "Trust in the Lord God with all your heart, remember him in everything you do, and he will show you the right way." "Love one another just as I have loved you." "Be strong and don't be afraid. God is coming to your rescue."

The celebration concludes with a final hymn "And the Father will dance", followed by tea and cakes and general happy chat. Those who were wandering around beforehand, nervously clutching bits of paper and saying, "I have to read a poem . . .", "I have to sing a song . . .", now relax. As a local man once pointed out, what is good about the celebrations is that you see people with gifts you did not know they had. That judgment is well borne out today. They may not be gifts that will make any sort of mark in the wider, competitive society of today's world; but for the local community they are gifts indeed, and those who have done something in the celebration surprise themselves by what they have achieved. As for religious content, the message that has come across is simple, basic and compelling: God takes care of us. We must love and trust. We are all brothers and sisters.

Night Prayer

Much later that night a small group of us goes up for Night Prayer, to the little chapel situated in one of the back bedrooms of a maisonette. There is a warm carpet, hessian-covered walls, a tabernacle – with a large plant and a lamp behind it, a white statue of Mary carrying the infant Jesus, a few comfortable chairs and some prayer-stools – which turn over to form simple bookcases. Through the window (when it is daylight) you can see another wing of the concrete block stretching before you.

Tonight we are nine – myself, Margaret Walsh, another Hope Community member, and six local people. We begin with a hymn from the Hope Community hymn-book (duplicated sheets of favourite music, held together at the spine with a strip of plastic).

Margaret asks us to remember the day we have just lived through, and to see what was special in it for each of us. There is a prayerful silence for a couple of minutes, before we each in turn share our thoughts. One man remembers his hot dinner, and how he had got up in front of all the people at the celebration to say they were welcome. The next person remembers being woken at five in the morning, and standing up to announce fire regulations at the celebration. Another remembers working the projector at the celebration, and how funny it was when people sang the verses in the wrong order. One woman has had an awful day. But her neighbour has had a perfect day, as every day is, but this one was special because of the celebration. Another remembers how the children were supposed to dance at the end of the celebration, but many were too shy. I remember Jim's image of the rainbow, and meeting a brother or sister on the bridge. And Margaret remembers a black woman she had met up with at the celebration and visited that night, to help put in her eye-drops: the woman cannot read and the hospital sent her home with four different bottles, which she could not tell apart, so Margaret has colour-coded them with a simple chart. We all give thanks for the day.

After another hymn, a local man reads a passage he has chosen from the Bible. He had asked earlier in the evening if there would be any scripture tonight and if he could help with Night Prayer, and Margaret had handed him a bible to look for something he would like to read. He had spent an hour searching, and had come back so excited to have found the story of the New Jerusalem near the end of the book. He did not know it was a famous reading, he just likes it and now he tells us why. At our celebration today, he says, everyone was there together – black and white, rich and poor, local people and visitors from other parts. All were there with one purpose – to worship God. If only it was always like that but, "This passage gives me hope that things are not as bad as sometimes they seem to be."

In the silence that follows this explanation, Margaret asks if anyone has a prayer or a hymn to follow that. How about the "Our Father", says one, and he himself leads it. Someone else suggests a hymn on the theme of glory at the end of time, but we do not know the tune so we read it aloud instead. Then we each pray for our concerns – for people who have left the estate, for the Gulf crisis, for the sick, "for myself" (says one) "because so many things lead me away from God, like drink and drugs, and I want to commit myself to God but I cannot". Margaret gives this person a final prayer to read for us all, from a book by Frank Topping:

> Take my life Lord, in spite of me . . . .
> Take my life and let it be,
> Consecrated, Lord, to thee.

We end this very special day with singing "Bind us together, Lord," and with the "Glory be".

Reflection

I asked Margaret if she saw the Hope Community as a basic Christian community. Her reply was modest and she hesitated to lay claim to that title, on various grounds. In the first place, not everyone who came was Christian. "To me a basic Christian community suggests a knowledge of the scriptures or at least a growing interest in the Word of God. Many of our people have not arrived there yet and maybe never will. Community – yes, I am quite happy with the whole concept of community and the scripture of life – the Word of God in those terms. Obviously some of our people want to find knowledge of the scriptures and of Christ, and it is happening all the time. But those associated with us come from all sorts of shades of belief."

Even "the option for the poor" is a phrase Margaret uses with discretion, because it can sound patronizing, as though to say, "you poor souls need our help". "They are all different and unique, each one of them with their own story, gifts and dreams. We deprive ourselves and society of the unique contribution which they can make, when we dismiss them with these soul-destroying labels."[9]

She also wonders whether the local community would ever reach the maturity to be called a basic Christian community. "It must be a different thing in the third world where most people are poor, and from among the poor you must have great potential. But we have not got that here and that is just a fact. With this policy of home care in the community we have got so many people who have left psychiatric hospital, and they are being housed in places like this. They have been chucked out of hospital and there are plenty of empty properties around here. At least half a dozen of the people who were here last night are on tablets or injections for 'nerves'."

Naturally that results in problems for any organized community activity: "When ten people sincerely intend to work on a project, we are lucky if half of them are able to turn up at the appointed time."[10] And so: "sometimes you think you are just doing nothing but carrying. You want to liberate, and enable, and empower, but a lot of our time is spent just being with and carrying people who are here. Maybe our grand plans for them will never work out, and they will never be truly independent or able to cope in the sense that we think they should be able to. The people with more ability tend to get out of the estate – if they can find the opportunity they are off – but some of them cannot. It has taken me a long time to accept that and I have not found it easy. People here have a lot of potential but it is not the kind of potential that enables them to cope with what life demands round here. So they easily drift to the margins and will stay there."

Despite Margaret's hesitations, I think there are good grounds for recognizing what is going on at the Hope Community as genuinely belonging to the process of basic Christian community. Basic Christian community, after all, is more a process than an achievement. If we compare the approach at Heath Town with that, for example, of Anne McSweeney at Osvaldo Manzanares *barrio*, we can really say the method is identical. Much of the work rightly is for the benefit of those with any religion or none, but there are also many occasions of explicit Christian sharing. A Christian community is found at the heart of a wider community that is open to all, irrespective of creed.

In talking of basic Christian community here, I am not speaking of the resident community of pastoral agents, any more than I would have been calling the three Maryknoll missioners who moved to Osvaldo Manzanares a base community. As I explained in chapter 2, "base community" is usually used of the local people, not of a residential community that pitches its tent among them. And so perhaps Margaret Walsh's three concentric circles should be seen as four, where the third is local Christians (however loosely defined) and the fourth is local people irrespective of creed.

The fact that the work is among "little ones" – many with mental health problems or caught in a habitual web of sin and failure – is a reminder that such people are every bit as much a part of the Church as those who are more independent. Basic ecclesial community is for everyone, however humble, not just for the more capable. Maybe the local community will develop beyond its early, fragile stage of dependency. Maybe it never will. Whichever way it is, Jesus surely has room for these people in his Church.

To say this, however, is to raise a dilemma. For the Hope Community is hesitant about promoting the sacraments, even baptism, without which, after all, no one is a member of the Church. Were they actively to encourage people to prepare for the sacraments, they would immediately have to choose which Church to baptize them into, which eucharistic table to gather them around. And if that question were forced, the Community would be in danger of losing its ecumenical neutrality. I was introduced to one woman from the estate who had recently received Catholic confirmation; but this would not have happened if the woman were not already a baptized Catholic, and had herself asked for it.

Theoretically it sounds like a contradiction, for the pastoral agents receive the support of the sacraments, while the people do not. The sisters go to mass at the local parish church, and an Anglican member of the Community worships at one of the Anglican churches. There is also a mass said by a priest who visits regularly to give support – but this is for the resident community, not for the local people.

And yet, in practice, at the Community's present stage of development, it is not experienced as a problem. For, says Margaret, although "many are expressing a desire to make a commitment to Christ and to belong to Christian community," none the less "they know that they would be unable to fulfil some of the promises made in our baptismal services or keep many of the other rules". She has given some thought to a pre-baptismal liturgy of commitment, which would stop short of the promises of baptism, and which, at the same time, would not favour one Christian denomination over the others. But that is as yet an area of exploration. What seems to be happening in practice is that the people express and renew some kind of commitment to Christ simply through their participation in the monthly celebrations and the daily prayer. And they do so at their own level, a level short of Church membership.

Can an ecumenical community be a basic cell of the Church, when people cannot join the Church through that community? I raise the issue in no way as a criticism, for the Hope Community calls itself neither a basic ecclesial community, nor a basic cell of the Church. But it does show that ecumenical base communities are not as straightforward and obvious as people sometimes assume. Later on we will look at a different way of trying to tackle the question of sacraments in an ecumenical setting, when we go to Liverpool to visit the Anfield Road Fellowship.

Despite these qualifications, we cannot fail to notice the many positive signs of basic Christian community at Heath Town, which are almost too numerous to mention. We may have been struck in the first place by the image of concentric circles to describe the levels of community. Then there are the clear signs of communion with the local churches, so that the work of the Hope Community is owned by the wider parishes, not seen as an alternative community.

We can notice how the cycle of See-Judge-Act-Celebrate-Evaluate has been followed through. Visiting people and listening to their stories has been the fundamental starting point for any work. There is a solidarity with the poor, a choice to live among them and see the world through their eyes, so that "you" becomes "we". There is an emphasis on enabling them to act for themselves, however limited and small such acts may have to be.

There is responsibility taken on for the locality, so that the Christian community is not an elite group but is at the service of all. And alongside the responsibility for the locality there is a solidarity with the poor elsewhere, wherever they may be. Community-building is expressed through the use of every opportunity to get people together, so that they meet in natural ways. Sharing is a prime value, as we see in the "shared table" and in many other ways. And through the growth of the community, people find their own dignity and discover their gifts. This is the heart of liberation.

The Christian message is expressed, in its most basic and fundamental form – a message of love and sharing. The Bible is read, and interpreted contextually. There is symbol and celebration – everything from birthdays to Christian liturgy. And the Christian liturgy is re-invented, echoing that phrase from Leonardo Boff: "the basic Christian communities re-invent the Church".

The final word goes to Margaret, in answer to the question whether she felt she had been evangelized by the poor. "I am far more evangelized by them than I evangelize," she said. And she explains how she has experienced that truth: "The Heath Town people abound in the gifts of the Spirit – in love, joy, peace, patience, goodness, kindness."[11] Because of that, "I am convinced that by listening to them, learning from them and by being creative in our response to meet their needs, the whole Church could be renewed. Many of our friends here are more free to explore new models of Church and of liturgy, since they are not bound by norms and conventions which others of us may find hard to abandon after years of practice."[12]

Margaret spoke quietly and with simple sincerity as she said to me, "I can reflect back on five and a half years and say with complete honesty that it has been the most formative time in the whole of my religious life. The whole message of powerlessness just became real, and it is easier to keep the focus on the values of the Gospel in a place like this. I think I have met the Jesus of the gospels here, Jesus of Nazareth, in a way that I have never known him before."

Chapter 9

STARTING FROM THE STREET:

The Anfield Road Fellowship

Most of the examples we have looked at have come from a Catholic background, but the Anfield Road Fellowship, by contrast, reflects a more Protestant evangelical tradition. "Fellowship" is a term popular in evangelical circles, and is often used of a church group that does not meet in a church building. It is a translation of the Greek word *koinonia*, more often rendered by Catholics as "communion". At Anfield Road, the term "community" is used of the members of the locality in general rather than the Christian community in particular.

Dave Cave is the principal moving force behind the Fellowship. He spoke to me at length about the Fellowship, during three visits I made to Anfield over a couple of years. He explained how, during the course of seventeen years as a United Reformed Church (URC) minister among the urban poor of Bradford and Liverpool,[1] he began to feel increasingly a "dissatisfaction with the structures of the institutional Church in meeting the needs, physical and spiritual, of those communities".

For the Church in urban areas, he said, money has always been a millstone. "One of the problems would be that you would have a building that was built for a bygone age, that would be large, cold and usually suffering – partly from age (so you would have dry rot and plaster peeling off the walls) and partly from vandalism (so you would have broken windows and lead removed from the roof). Church buildings in the inner city often become like fortresses – barbed wire on the fences, and locked and bolted except for services."

The second great drain on local finances was the support of a minister. Many urban-poor congregations could not afford a minister of their own and had to share one between several churches.

Another problem about paying a minister is that it implies putting most leadership tasks onto one person in such a way that the laity feel they can opt out and become armchair Christians.

Another major problem "is movement of congregation, because in every tradition what has tended to happen is that as people have been able to achieve – financially, educationally, etc. – they have moved out of the poorer areas. So what will happen in the first generation is somebody will move a few miles up the road, but they will still come back to their parish church or their local chapel. The problem is that they are no longer authentic members of the community, and they will then very often be the ones who are made the leaders, actually making decisions on behalf of the community they no longer represent. In the second generation, some will stick through loyalty but the majority will not. So then you get a dropping congregation. What you eventually get over a period of years is a group of very elderly people, and gradually that church gets to the point that it closes. Over the last fourteen years in Liverpool I have seen churches of every tradition struggling with these issues, and closing down, and regrouping, and not really making a serious, radical response to the situation."

So in 1983 Dave, together with his wife Tina, their two young boys Gareth and Merfyn, and his cousin Wendy, moved into a Victorian terraced house on the Anfield Road in Liverpool. There, with the help of an original core of seven local Christians, they started an inner-city outreach project that *did* aim to be a radical response to the problems.

(INNER CITY OUTREACH PROJECT)

It is one of the roughest areas of the city, hard by the Shankly gates of the famous Liverpool football club – "the finest football team in the country, and we suspect in Europe". The gates bear the legend "You'll never walk alone" – words which "mean one thing to the football fans – but a great deal more to us as Christians".[2]

"When Anfield was begun," Dave explained, "we said firstly, we would not own any buildings": the Fellowship was to happen in peoples' houses. "Secondly, we would not pay any ministry. It seemed almost an anathema that, in an area with really high unemployment, we should look for money to pay somebody to do something, when people had time on their hands": the Caves were to be supported by Tina's salary as a hospital haematologist. "Because we do not depend on money we are actually liberated: people who give you money control you." Thirdly, "recognizing the problems of travelling congregations, we have actively discouraged anybody who does not live within walking distance from the Liverpool football stadium from being a part of our Fellowship. Last year we referred seventeen people to other churches, who had heard about us and felt they would like to join us, but were not from this community."

For the founder members of the Fellowship there were two images that captured their vision. "One was a very biblical one. Somebody preaching one day talked about Jesus needing a donkey to take him into the city of Jerusalem, and needing donkeys to take him into cities today. We felt that we were called to be the donkeys, and to take the name of Jesus back onto the streets of the poor areas and the poor communities."

The other image was "the picture of the grit in the oyster. The grit in an oyster causes aggravation, inflammation and irritation, but eventually produces a pearl. We were to cause the aggravation, the irritation and the inflammation in the Church, but with the ultimate intention of producing the pearl of great price."

By this time Dave had already heard of Latin American basic ecclesial communities, and "We began to read about them with more and more enthusiasm because they had more of an authentic ring about them, in the way they were responding to issues, than anything we had experienced in Western Christianity." But at first he suspected "that the one thing that would stop Anfield having any authentic identification with what was going on there, was that I am a professional, ordained clergyman": from what he had heard, it sounded as though the Latin American base communities had sprung up spontaneously from the people at the bottom without any clerical involvement. It was only "later, when I went over to Latin America and saw for myself, that I began to become more and more aware that there were no indigenous groups that sprang up totally on their own. There was always some kind of enabler."

Dave explained, "We did not set out to ape a base community model", but as he found out more about base communities around the world, he realized more and more "that the journey we were making, in many respects, had a lot of parallels with the experiences of these other groups".

The locality

Dave gave me a guided tour of the locality when I visited him. There was a block of flats where IRA bomb factories have been found before now. A house with no windows was pointed out as a site where drug addicts go for fixes. The local vicar had had a petrol bomb thrown at his house because he opposed the drug-taking on a neighbouring estate. I asked Dave about unemployment levels, and he said "if you take out government schemes, it is over 90 per cent among the young people".

We went down a back street, where dustbin bags were lying, broken open, all over the road: the rubbish is only collected every three weeks or so, Dave said, and the rats and cats fight over it, while cockroaches infect the houses. He pointed out to me a couple of "red light" houses, and a shop that was boarded up against thieves.

Street kids were everywhere – playing in the road or just ambling about, not knowing what to do. Some of them were climbing on the wall of a house that was run by the Fellowship for ex-prisoners: that too had boarded-up windows for security. Several houses on the Anfield Road had recently been subjected to arson attacks from street gangs, and some insurance companies would not insure cars or property in the Anfield area at all.

Street kids, Dave explained, "typically come from a broken home situation. They will have truanted from the age of eleven or twelve, and they will generate an income from stealing. They will often entertain themselves by stealing cars for the excitement of joy-riding. They then progress to dabbling with drugs to cope with boredom. It usually starts with cannabis, or sniffing things like glue, fire extinguishers, aerosols, lighter fuel: young people experiment to see which ones they can get a lift from and sometimes they kill themselves. It is very sad. Then they will quite often use forms of LSD – the most popular one round here now is ecstasy. And then they will progress to something like heroin". The majority of the hundred or so local street kids, said Dave, were heroin addicts.

Every attempt to improve the area seemed to have gone wrong. There was a new housing estate built, on the model of a Cornish fishing village, with charming little nooks and crannies: but it had provided a paradise for muggers, and had to be demolished. Then there was a local park, with little hills: it might seem a welcome stretch of green, but the Cave boys had both been beaten up in the local parks. For Dave and Tina to bring their own children to live in such an environment was a decision we can either admire, or regard as wildly irresponsible: I prefer to admire it.

Finally, as we reached a crossroads, we saw an Orange march go by in full swing. Faces were shining with pride and focused in concentration, as these Protestant extremists marched and played in rhythm with their drums and pipes, adorned in colourful banners and sashes. Dave shook his head sadly. "I have no time for anything that is founded on hatred," he said.

Another member of the Fellowship to whom I spoke at length was Andy Dawson. He was born and bred in Anfield, though he is now studying in Oxford, and he told me, "It is a fairly tough place to grow up, and it is a very tough place to live if you have not grown up there, very tough. Dave is always having people who say, 'I've read about you in this book. I want to come and work in Anfield; I want to come and live here,' and Dave will try his level best to put them off. We find with the people who have come in, they suddenly realize what life in Anfield is like. Walking out in the night you are risking getting mugged, beaten up or raped. Or the chances of your house being robbed are very, very high. Dave was stripped of £2,000 worth of stuff from his house a couple of months ago: they just kicked in the front door on one of the busiest roads in Anfield and they stripped the house in a matter of fifteen minutes. My Mum and Dad's house has been broken into seven or eight times. That which is not nailed down or screwed down goes. Asking the kids who are involved in crime to justify themselves, they say, 'Why shouldn't I have it if they have it?' Or 'What goes around comes around. I steal from them, they steal from us'."

The make-up of the Fellowship

The original seven members were all contacts made at the Rock Church in adjacent Everton, where Dave had been minister up until the move. They were local people, says Dave, "who for a variety of reasons were struggling with traditional Church spirituality. We said we would not want to cause any split: they would only be acceptable as part of this new group if they had the blessing of the leadership, which they duly gave."

Andy Dawson was one of these indigenous, seven founder

members, and was sixteen years old at the time the Fellowship started. He left school with one "O" level and went to work as a labourer in the building trade until he was made redundant. But Christianity changed his perspective on education, and in due course Andy gained "O" levels, then "A"s, then a first-class degree in Theology, and a masters in Chicago, with a thesis on "The relevance and challenge of the Latin American base ecclesial community experience for the Western Church in an urban milieu". At the time of writing he is working on a doctorate in Oxford, after which he is due to be ordained as a URC minister.

From the original seven, the Fellowship began to grow almost at once. The first new arrival was Graham, a seventeen-year-old drug addict and pusher, who had been in constant trouble with the police. He had begun to feel his life challenged through the influence of Christians, but he did not know how to handle this, and the Christians he knew did not know how to handle him. A woman from a local Baptist church brought him round one night at midnight. Dave reports: "I sat up and eventually he went home, but was back bright and early for our Sunday morning meeting. During the meeting some of us laid hands on Graham . . . and our first new convert joined Anfield Road in the second week of its existence."[3]

Graham taught himself to read and write the basic letters so he could read his Bible. "His contacts were tremendous," said Andy, "Who he didn't know wasn't worth knowing in Anfield. When people suddenly saw the change in his life – he stopped dealing in drugs, he stopped taking drugs, he stopped involving himself in crime, though occasionally he did have his odd laughs – they wanted to know why. And he would say, 'Come along, come along to Friday evening, the youth session.' So it was chock-a-block with kids: sometimes they were taking things and were high at the time, other kids were not. That is how we got known in the community, just by word of mouth. I think the vital thing was just being there in Anfield, going into the shops, or signing on at the social security office and speaking to other people." (Note, however, that Dave does not sign on for the dole as he is not available for employment.)

In the Caves' own house the bottom two floors are available for Fellowship use, while the family have their bedrooms and a private sitting-room on the upper floors. The Caves have also let their guest room be used, on a number of occasions, by those coming off drugs. Maps on a notice board in the hall show the different places all over the world from which visitors have come. The front room is the "meeting room", used for Sunday worship, and general socializing: it has a piano, and looks just like an ordinary lounge, with lots of comfy seating. The family kitchen is used once a week for a lunch club, providing cheap, nutritious meals and company, mainly for single men.

Down in the basement is a snooker table, used by the youth who come in for open house on Sunday nights. The Caves operate a rule of the "4Ss" inside the house – "no smoking, no swearing, no stealing, and no spitting" – and it works well. Tina told me they had never had anything stolen: the only thing she had ever noticed go missing was a tape, and when she asked about it, it was returned a few days later.

But the members of the Fellowship are in and out of each other's houses all the time, so it really is a multi-site community. In addition to the Sunday worship, there are four Bible study groups that meet during the week – all in different homes. The youth group has a Bible study session they run just for themselves during the week, in addition to one that is led by an adult. On Monday morning there is a leaders' meeting, attended by three men and one woman.

An interesting use of language is that "going to church" is used of a meeting in someone's house. The people have even developed for themselves the phrase "having Church". In this way, they show they have really come to understand that the Church is the believers gathered together, in no way to be confused with a building.

There are now about fifty members of the Fellowship, including both Protestants and Catholics. As Dave showed me photos of past social events, he told me about the lives of the various individuals that have been part of the Fellowship at one time or another. One was a former heroin pusher, and the next a social worker; one a nurse, and the next an ex-alchoholic; one was now in prison, and the next a bank clerk. Andy says, "People with problems just materialize. More than 50 per cent have problems which you or I would deem major, I suppose, like drug addiction, alcoholic abuse . . . . Money problems is a very big one, and it might drive you to certain things – one of them is prostitution."

Outreach

Dave explains some of the outreach work connected with the Fellow-ship: "Over the years we've developed work with the homeless, and in association with Adullam Homes we operate two houses in this area. We have also been working very hard on a community house, where we could bring people from a background of mental handicap back into the community." On my last visit, there was much excite-ment about a drop-in coffee shop which opened in July 1991, and gives street kids somewhere to go. The first coffee is free but sub-sequent drinks should be paid for. This is a joint venture, together with the local Baptists, Anglicans and Methodists, though the initiat-ive came from the Fellowship.

The coffee shop project has been prayed over with some liturgical creativity. One night, Dave recounts, after a Bible study on how Nehemiah went about building up his ruined city, someone said, "What are we going to do about it?" And so "a gang of us ended up going out onto Walton Breck Road at ten at night, as the pubs were beginning to empty, and anointing a shop doorpost with oil and praying. It was a vacant shop at that time, and we were praying that God would supply us with a vacant shop. We got some very strange looks from some of the local residents walking down the road, thinking that we had now finally flipped. As it happened we ended up getting the shop across the road from there."

A little later on, someone leading a Sunday evening meeting brought along a bag containing a paintbrush, a saucepan, a set of keys, and things like that; and asked everybody to take something that represented the contribution they felt they could make to the coffee shop. One man immediately took out the paintbrush because he felt he could help decorate the coffee shop and get it ready. "There was even a teddy bear, and someone grabbed that because they felt they would like to help look after any children who came in. People were beginning to commit themselves."

On Saturday 15 April 1989, a terrible disaster struck Anfield, when ninety-five Liverpool football fans were crushed to death in an overcrowding accident at Hillsborough ground in Sheffield, during an "away" game. Living right next door to the home ground, the members of the Fellowship shared in the grief and solidarity of the local people, which expressed itself in almost liturgical ways. The Caves wrote to their friends in a prayer letter of May 1989:

"Especially affected has been the Anfield area, where Liverpool FC's ground has been a place of pilgrimage for over a million people, who have come to pay tribute with flowers and other tokens, and to express the grief and shock we have all felt. We've seen grown men crying openly in the street and in the stands and terraces, and mothers and children – some with a grim absence of husbands and sons." On the Saturday following the disaster the Fellowship opened one of their houses to "those who wanted to come and talk, over a cup of tea," collaborating with other local churches in offering a listening ear. "Probably the most requested facility was the loo!" but one man came in "and sobbed his heart out for an hour".

Evaluating

"Part of the journey," says Dave, "is that we made loads and loads of mistakes, but we always sat down and thought them through and had another go. And we became more and more aware that this was one of the big differences between us and the more traditional Christian communities in this country. They want everything signed, sealed and delivered before they will have a go at it. My youngest son used to say, 'I don't like this' and 'I don't like that', and when asked, 'Why not?' he would say, 'Because I've never tried it'. I think that reflects some of the thinking of the Church some-times. Whereas we developed a policy of 'have a go', and if it doesn't work out, don't weep over it, learn from it. And by doing that we progressed."

What mistakes had they made? "One of the things we did at the beginning was we made a number of rules. And every time we made a rule, someone came along and challenged that rule. In the end we said, we won't have rules in future we'll have principles. They are guiding, and they are not rigid, because at the end of the day people come first. We learned this from Jesus, from the story when he talked about the sabbath." For example, "one of the rules we made was that nobody who did not live within Anfield could be a member of our community. Then someone came along who was schizophrenic, with real dependency needs, and related quite closely to Tina. We thought, 'Well, the person is much more important than the rule,' so we broke the rule."

Another example was that "we started in the early days with quite a chauvinistic approach – leadership is male. That was a reflection of the culture as we saw it, and we would justify it by saying, 'If we are going to reach out to the community we have got to reflect the culture, and therefore to affirm male leadership would be the way to do it.' But as time went by you looked at it realistically and it just was not true. We discovered that although men are always quite happy to take positions where they can wear a badge and say, 'I'm a leader', if you were looking for the activists, the people who were the real enablers in the community, it was the women. The women were the better community organizers. Women were the better communicators in the grapevines of the community. Women were better at organizing everything, from food to finance. And the more we developed, the more we realized that the most authentic leadership within our Fellowship was actually women. And so there again, where we had made almost a rule at the beginning, it then became a principle, and then went out of the window, because over a period of time we did almost a total reversal on that."

Another example of a mistake was "we got to the point in our development where we felt the need for deacons – people who would take on some of the practical aspects, if somebody needed a room decorating or a fence repairing. So we did a lot of Bible study on it, and people's names were put forward and they were appointed. And we had laboured very hard in teaching that they would be servants of the Fellowship, not bosses. And then we had our first meeting, and it was like they had been made monitors or prefects at school. It was quite frightening in a way. But what was interesting was we only ever had two meetings, because the folks themselves realized what it was doing to them. So without ever anyone actually officially saying anything, the whole thing disintegrated and nobody ever wanted to appoint deacons again."

Leadership

If the deacons' experiment did not work out, there are plenty of other leadership roles that did, showing that the people are being truly liberated and empowered. "You will normally hear people tell you," says Dave, "that in urban areas there is no real, authentic, local leadership, and therefore that the professionals have to struggle on, on their own. And yet if you take a Fellowship here of just over fifty, including children, we have actively fourteen people who take Bible study groups, who lead worship, and who preach; eight of them men and six women. All of them are home-grown, and all have operated the apprenticeship model."

By the apprenticeship model Dave means that "You have an 'old hand' who has an apprentice by them, to whom they give the chance to do small jobs, and then bigger jobs, until eventually they have served their time. That is always something that we have done in worship, for instance: we will always make sure that an 'old hand' is around to help and encourage the person through. And just like the apprentice, they will have a go and they will make a mess of it on occasions. But nobody rubs their nose in it and there is no negative response from the rest of the community. Some people show absolutely no ability and so they tend not to be asked to do things again, but other people have the spark that encouraged can grow into a flame."

"In the early days of Anfield Road," Dave admits, "I was a one-man band. When we first began I would preach, I would lead worship, I would play the music, I would do the Bible study and I did virtually everything. But as time went by we began to encourage other people to participate." After seven years of pursuing the apprenticeship model, "not only have we sent folk out to other places, but we have maintained a level of leadership at the local level that means that I am actually only active in worship on average about once a month."

There are, however, " what you would almost call sacramental roles that people would look in my direction for. If we have a believers' baptism, I would normally be expected to do that. Or if we had an infant dedication, I would normally be expected to do that. Or if somebody in the Fellowship gets married, I would normally be expected to do that. Communion is not quite so rigid: I would preside over the breaking of the bread, but when it actually comes to breaking the bread I would ask people to come and do it. Or I would ask people to pass it round, or pass the cup round, and get people to feel that this is as much their communion as mine."

Wendy, Dave's cousin, points out there are problems about getting other people to sustain leadership. "They can do a meeting, fine; a Bible study or whatever. But the moment people take on projects there comes a stage, which always disappoints me, when they don't feel like it any more. That is something I struggle with here, because you start something and there is a terrific wave of enthusiasm, and then something goes wrong or the impetus is lost and people start to drop out, and it is all the incomers who are left to pick up the pieces." (The use of the term "incomer" is similar to what is sometimes called an "external pastoral agent", that is, someone who is not indigenous to the community but comes in from the outside to enable community development.) Wendy continues, laughing but half-serious: "Tina and I never volunteer for anything, because we know we will always get it in the end. And the people who are really committed tend to go away, like Andy and Debbie, who have really got the stamina and the commitment to see something through."

Dave agrees, and refers back to what he was saying earlier about base communities around the world all needing an enabler. "It is naïve to say, if you take that person out of the situation, it will carry on. That is the theory that has been produced, and the reality is that it is not true, and you have to accept that there has to be someone there to maintain the vision. We always thought the base community movement was highly motivated and organized, but the more I have met people around the world the more I have found that they are just like our lot. If you have not got one or two incomers into the situation to facilitate them, they would all crumble and fall to pieces. So I feel more an authentic part of a base community than I did five years ago, because of what I have seen elsewhere."

Dave recognizes that the people in Anfield work with short-term goals, "so you try and gear the Fellowship to short-term goals, and build on that, rather than try and impose something on them that is not their natural way of doing things. If somebody wants to go on a conference, you have to anticipate that six months in advance, because by the time our folks decide they want to go, these things are fully booked. So what you do is take a 'guesstimate' and book that number of places. Sometimes it is only days before, or even on the day, that people decide they want to go."

During their years in urban ministry, the Caves can count seventeen people who have gone on to train for mission elsewhere. Apart from Andy and his wife Debbie, others from Anfield Road have gone on to theological college at Cambridge, to the Methodist Association of Youth Clubs, to inner-city ministry in Manchester, to work with the mentally handicapped, and so on. Most have returned to an institutional framework for their training, which might seem paradoxical after the insights of a more radical way of working. But it illustrates their principle of being grit in the oyster, rather than opting out to run their own show.

One of the Fellowship members, a young man in his twenties called Steve, who comes from the worst estate in the Anfield area, told me what a shame it was that candidates for ministry were taken out of their environment and sent to college, so they lost their class base. When they came back from several years in a college, even their accent tended to sound posh in the ears of the locals, however regional it might sound to standard-English ears. If you sounded like an outsider, said Steve, you were less able to reach local, working-class people, and to take the Gospel to where they were, in the pub or whatever. "It is useless sitting in church waiting for people to come."

Steve is one of a small group involved in a more local experiment, based on the Anfield Road model rather than on a traditional congregation. The Valley Christian Fellowship made a hesitant beginning in 1990, half a mile down the road. Whether or not this comes to anything, Dave explains, the vision is "to have lots of small Christian communities that will radiate out on an amoeba principle from each other, and be independent of each other but related to each other". We are reminded of the "cell" imagery with which this book began.

Marginalization

Some grassroots social analysis has been done by the Fellowship, in a report called "Marginalization: A View from the Underside",[4] which they prepared for the European Base Communities' Conference in Paris, 1991. (Dave, however, sees some differences between Anfield Road and many of the European groupings. At a former European base communities' congress in Bilbao he found, "what they called base communities was not what we were doing. Most of the groups we met, which were from places like Italy and Holland and Spain and France, were essentially middle-class in their make-up. They did not have the feel about them that ours did, and they seemed to be much more along the lines of political activists than genuine, authentic community activity. It is fair enough to do that, but it was not what we were at. Again, our understanding of base community was to take a fresh look at biblical principles and apply them practically into our own situations, and there was virtually none of that.") Dave absented himself from the process of preparing the report, so there would no danger of him exerting undue influence. Bill Bullin, from the Evangelical Urban Training Project, came as facilitator, working with the three different Bible study groups over several weeks, and compiling the findings.

The report begins by asking, "What do we think 'marginalization' means?" "We were not sure," came the answer, "but we had heard other people talk about it. We thought about the margin we used to rule on a piece of paper at school. Putting to the side. Putting people into boxes. Pushing people out. Out-casting people. Making some people 'second class citizens'. Making people feel worthless." (See p. 176.)

Within different geographical areas, they noticed, different sorts of people are marginalized. Within Anfield itself, the people who are looked down on are "middle-class, educated, police, car-owners, and Pakis". But in Liverpool as a whole the marginalized are "blacks, Asians, Catholics, and addicts". And in Britain the marginalized include "single parents, gays, elderly, mentally-handicapped and the North".

As they pursued the meaning of marginalization, one comment that came out was that people "feel angry about businessmen coming up from the South; taking over factories, promising people their jobs will be OK, making them unemployed a short time later and knocking down the factory. Then they sell the land to someone like Barretts (a large, national building company) for private housing." Another comment was, "The people at the bottom know what it is

We thought of several different ways of talking about and drawing the idea of "MARGINALISATION":

"Pushed Aside"

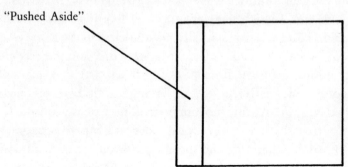

"Left Out"

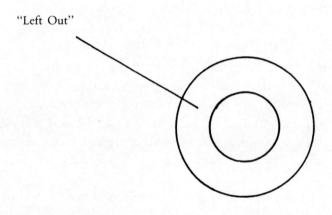

"Looked Down On"

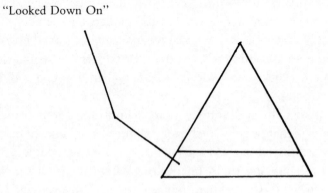

like for people at the top, but people at the top don't know what it's like for people at the bottom." So the Anfield gang explain for themselves what it feels like at the bottom:

What is Bad for the Outcasts?
No money.
Poor housing.
Difficulties in marriage.
Poor health – you don't live as long.
Poorer education.
Unemployment.
Escapism i.e. drugs.
Having to rely on the State.

What is Good for the Outcasts?
It brings you closer to your family and friends.
It makes you more generous and hospitable.
More free time.
Slower pace of life.
Don't have to get up in the mornings.
You are less materialistic – it can make you more spiritual.

The Church, too, came under criticism for marginalizing people in the pew:

We thought about old-fashioned classrooms. (Most churches are like old-fashioned school classrooms.)
"You sit in rows."
"One person at the front."
"Set, rigid rules."
"Some people can't keep up."
"There's no freedom to express yourself."
"It's boring."

Anfield Road is different.
"More freedom."
"More creative."
"More open."
"It brings out more in you."

"You can relate to people."

"You have a choice."

But there were problems too:

"There can be poor communication."

"It can lack structure."

"There can be too much freedom."

"It can lack order."

A number of scripture passages were used to throw light on their experience of marginalization. There was the saying from Matthew 20, "The first shall be last and the last first", the parable of the pharisee and the tax collector, and the workers in the vineyard. But the key passage they turned to – without knowing that it was a favourite of Latin American liberation theologians – was the oppression of the Israelites in the book of Exodus.

Worship and scripture

The regular worship as a Fellowship is on Sunday mornings, and once a month this is a eucharist. They keep it to a monthly celebration, so that anyone who has problems about eucharistic sharing can miss that meeting without embarrassment – or they can simply pass on the bread without partaking, and some do that too. The last thing Dave wants is for the eucharist to cause division. Some members attend churches of their own denomination as well, but for most, the Fellowship meeting is their only form of worship.

Andy remembers a number of people coming in to the Caves' front lounge, looking round and saying:

"Where is the church?"

"Well, we meet here of a Sunday morning."

"You sit on a couch?!" And they'll bounce up and down on the couch and say, "No, you're kidding me, it's downstairs."

And so, says Andy, "you'll take them downstairs and show them the snooker room, and it takes ages to convince people that you can sit on a couch in worship. That automatically breaks down images and presuppositions and prejudices."

The reading of scripture is very contextual at Anfield. Steve told me that "in the Bible I find nothing I cannot follow – except the names. But the books that try to explain the Bible, tend to take away from it rather than add. They make it more difficult to understand, not easier." Gradually the people have become aware that God has a special love for the poor, for those who are put down or marginalized in society. David Sheppard – the Anglican Bishop of Liverpool – brought out a book called *Bias to the Poor*, and though the Anfield Christians had not actually read the book, they knew about it and were affirmed by it. "It excited our folks that God is actively working in their favour," said Dave. "They had been presented in the past with a Gospel for the rich, but the more they actually read the Bible they discovered that it was good news for the poor."

I asked Andy if the ordinary people were able to join in on the interpretation of scripture. He replied, "Oh yes, you try and stop them. Because the whole ethos of the place is very informal, people tend to have a very relaxed attitude when they approach the Bible, and they are not afraid of saying, 'That could be me', 'That person is me'. You're in the middle of a sermon and someone puts his hand up. And you say, 'What, John?' And he'll say, 'Can I ask a question?' So trying to get people not to join in is an impossible task. I dread preaching there: you get an ability to hide behind a lectern or in a pulpit – there is a certain security there. But when you are in a room just a bit bigger than this, and you stand in the middle and you step over legs and you are trying to preach!"

He recalled a sermon he had to tape before going to college. "I was trying to use an analogy of creation – how creation is, in certain senses, ordered – and I talked about the peacock and I said it was male. Then Brian jumps up: 'No it's not, the peacock is female.' And everyone says, 'Shut up Brian, of course the peacock is male.' And this went on for ten minutes. And I had to sit down while everyone argued about whether the peacock is male or female."

I shared in worship one Sunday. There were twenty-six present that day, including six children, and the room was comfortably packed. Merfyn Cave operated the overhead projector, to throw the words of hymns onto a white sheet over the mantelpiece. We began with several hymns of praise, accompanied by two guitars. A teenage girl said a spontaneous prayer, and then someone read a passage from

Isaiah. After three more hymns there was "share time", which Dave has described as "a bit like the wife who asks her husband if he has had a good day at work – sharing is a family experience".[5] Today there were notices about a Christmas party, about the Valley Fellowship, about a funeral, and about friends who were ill. Straight after that, the children were taken out to do some artwork in the kitchen, and we sang three more hymns, this time about our response to God, like "I have decided to follow Jesus."

Then Gareth, aged sixteen, preached, sitting on the floor. He began by showing on the overhead projector a diagram of a football pitch. He asked someone to read Judges 7:17–25, about Gideon's battle against the host of Midian, and he talked us through the reading as though it were about a football match: "Here are the tactics", "This is what happened in the game" and "Here is the trophy coming up". Then he asked what made a good football team: "How do Liverpool win and Everton don't?". A mentally-handicapped man called Garry replied, "One, two, three, boo hoo," referring to Liverpool's recent 1–3 defeat by Arsenal. From the discussion Gareth concluded that in the top teams there is more control, a better manager, better preparation, stronger and more disciplined players, and that as a Church we can learn from this example how to work together better as a team.

Another hymn followed, and then the person leading the service asked Garry to step forward and pretend to be God: Garry looked pleased as punch. Now he asked two others to stand next to him. Garry gathered them both together in a big hug. "There you see, if we draw near to God, we draw near also to each other." The next hymn continued the theme of closeness to God, and I watched the mother of a new-born baby singing it lovingly, gazing into the eyes of her child:

> Within the veil I now would come
> Into the Holy Place to look upon thy face.

We ended with some prayers – for an epileptic boy who is in danger of setting fire to his house, for a local boy arrested in the Heysel football riot who has since become a Christian ("Good, good" said Garry), for the local café project run by the churches. Finally we stood and sang "Rejoice, rejoice, rejoice" ("Bad, bad" said Garry at everyone who was not clapping) and then joined hands for the grace. Just as we had finished, we heard drums and music, and looked out of the front window to see the local Orange Lodge marching its way along the Anfield Road.

Relationship to other Churches

The relationship of the Fellowship to other Churches is an interesting and a complex question. It is a crucial issue in a city where, according to Andy, everyone is "either Protestant (which means Anglican), or Catholic". When you say you are URC or Non-Conformist, they say, "Are you a non-conformist Protestant or a non-comformist Catholic?"

"We have developed ecumenically in all sorts of directions," says Dave, "some of which seem a contradiction in terms. On one side we joined the Evangelical Alliance, as somewhere where we could say we have an affiliation and belong to a wider grouping of Churches. We felt that we could go along with their statement of faith, even if they do include (though we struggle with them) very right-wing, fundamentalist groups. On the other side, we work very closely with the Bishop and Archbishop of Liverpool:[6] we are in regular correspondence and we have their support and encouragement. Then we have developed affiliations through the base community movement, also through urban networks."

There are excellent relations with the local Anglican, Catholic, Methodist and Baptist churches, on everything from joint Christmas cards to Christian counselling projects and the drop-in coffee bar. The Fellowship borrows local Free Church buildings for the celebration of weddings, and uses the baptistery of the Baptist church for believers' baptism.

"When we first began," Dave explained, "the local churches all viewed us with a great deal of suspicion because they thought we were a house church. And they had lost members of their congregations to house churches." But over the years they discovered "that we were ministering to a kind of folk they can't minister to: we operate what we call a Heineken ministry – we aim to reach those people other Churches cannot reach."

I asked Dave about how he saw the relationship of basic Christian communities to house churches. (This is a question often asked by those who have noticed the points they have in common – an informal style of worship, a freedom from clergy and building and institution, and a basis among people at the grassroots.) What would he say if someone asked if the Fellowship was a house church? His answer was a clear and immediate "no": the Fellowship is not part of the house church movement, "because it is not triumphalistic . . . because it is not into the prosperity ethic . . . because it is not charismatic, in the sense of swinging from the chandeliers."

Shortly after it started in 1983, the Fellowship formally applied to the URC for recognition as a congregation. The decision was negative, on two grounds. One was that the Anfield Road Fellowship was not prepared to baptize infants, Dave and others being strong proponents of believers' baptism, whereas in every URC congregation the minister must be prepared to baptize infants if requested to do so. However, there can be a conscience clause, that permits the minister to ask in another minister to perform the baptism if he does not believe in it himself.

The other point at issue was that, at that time, the Fellowship was not prepared to recognize the ministry of women. In the URC, where women can be ordained, it is vital that every congregation is prepared in principle to consider either a male or a female minister,[7] and to accept men or women as elders. We may be prompted to reflect that conservative ideas are not found only in institutions, riddled with bureaucracy and reluctance to change: on occasions it can be the institution – with its broader perspective – that struggles to overcome conservative ideas found at the grassroots.

But as we saw above, the Fellowship has done "almost a total reversal" on the position of women. It began in small ways, with encouraging the boys to let the girls have a go on the snooker table, and the men to share in the washing-up and even the cooking for the lunch club. By the time of my most recent visit, women and girls were leading Bible studies and worship and preaching, inclusive-language versions of Christmas carols were being used, and there was talk of "person-power".

At the time the rejection was painful but, instead of going off in a huff, the Fellowship stayed as close as it could to the URC by becoming an Associated Fellowship rather than a full member congregation. Dave explained: "One of the things I love about the Roman Catholic Church, as I have looked at it internationally, is no matter who goes off and does what, they find a way of including them. If necessary they create a new religious order, so no matter how much strain there is, they still come under an umbrella."

But over the years the URC has become very proud of its maverick, Associated body. It "now brings international delegates to look at Anfield Road as an example of what the URC is doing. Just in this last year they have brought people from the Council for World Mission here, from as far as New Zealand and Taiwan and India, to look at what we are doing."

I asked if the Fellowship would make a renewed application, now that the women's issue appears to have been resolved. Dave thought not. "When we made our application before it was because we never consciously wanted to be outside the URC. Part of the book of rules was that if it was a new congregation then it would have to apply for membership of the URC, not assume it as of right." But with the passage of years he doubts if it would be possible to go into the URC now, not for any doctrinal reasons, but because "forty per cent of the Fellowship would have Roman Catholic roots. If Anfield Road became a recognized URC church we would then have to have a URC membership, and that would divide people, because some people would become members and a lot of people would not. It would force people to make decisions that were culturally unfair – if somebody came from a Roman Catholic background they would have to effectively revoke their traditional faith and upbringing."

Andy, however, takes a slightly different line. "I would like to see it in the long run. Not only is it going to get its foot in the door, it is going to get its whole self behind the door, and it can have a lot more to say as regards Church action in the inner city." I asked about the dangers of being controlled, and Andy said, "Control is a pejorative term. A certain amount of answerability needs to be kept. There's a place where you can go for help. Also it gives you a channel, where you can feed in what you are experiencing. Just going it alone helps sometimes, but I think it hinders more."

On the question of whether first-world base communities should be ecumenical, Andy replied, "Ecumenical in ethos, ecumenical in practice, but ecumenical does not have to mean non-denominational in any sense." And he pointed out that many non-denominational churches, of the "house-church" or "community-church" variety (which are middle-class, with huge congregations driving in from a large area, and a very authoritarian and dogmatic manner), are very anti-ecumenical.

I asked Andy how he saw the shape of the Church to come. "Given the obvious secularization that has been undergone in the last couple of hundred years, I don't see there is going to be any mass revival of religion. I think what we are going to see is a denominational structure that is going to become smaller and far more voluntary than it tends to be now. The future of the Church is going to be more and more in smaller groups – instead of one large parish church, a group of five or six smaller communities in a large area; with one or two full-time ministers or enablers or pastors or whatever you want to call them travelling between them; and trying to enable people to use their own talents and use what they have got. I think that is going to be the future of the Church in this country, and I want to be involved in preparing the Church for the future it is going to meet, not trying to hold onto a past that has gone and is not going to come back."

Reflection

We have seen how base community influence permeated Dave's thinking from the start, and how his understanding of Anfield Road's relationship to third-world groups developed. I asked Andy too, whose thesis in Chicago had been on base communities, whether he thought the Anfield Road Fellowship was a basic Christian community. He replied: "I believe it is base in the sense that it is involved in the grassroots of the pyramidal structure of society. It is at the bottom, among the socio-economically deprived. Yes, I would say it is an embryonic grassroots community. I would even go so far as to say it is an embryonic base ecclesial community."

"I think for me," he said, "one of the notions of a base community is creating a space where people feel they can talk. At times they can be extremely serious and talk, and at other times they can just talk and know they'll be heard, and know what they say will be accepted. I think if Anfield has ever been a success at anything it has been a success at creating space, where people with an awful lot of problems can just come and talk and relax and share."

Anfield has very many points of identification with basic ecclesial communities that we could add to Andy's points, and they will have been evident throughout the report. Here we need only a brief summary.

Right from the original vision, Anfield was to show that the Church is not the building or the clergy, but the people. The "people" does not mean a self-selecting group, coming from far and wide to a community they like, but the ordinary people who live there. Leaders were not to be a privileged class, but leadership was to emerge from the people, according to talents and needs. And that is not to deny the need for a pastoral agent, coming in to act as leaven in the dough of the community.

The pastoral cycle is well represented at Anfield. The experience of the downtrodden is the starting point, and it is analysed, not just taken as the way things are or the will of God. The report on marginalization is an excellent example of the simple, direct social analysis that comes from the people themselves. The scriptures are always in people's thoughts, and they are read through the eyes of local experience. The "Act-Evaluate" sequence is what Dave calls "have a go, make mistakes, and learn from them". Celebration is evident too, and if the worship is perhaps more based on singing and less on symbolic action then some Catholic liturgies, all elements are still to be found there – as on the night when the people went out to pour oil on a shop doorpost.

The "amoeba principle" is the same ecclesiological concept as the Latin American "basic cell of the Church". There is, of course, a dilemma about whether the community can be a basic cell of the Church without being a basic cell of any denomination; but this is lived out as an on-going challenge and question, with no pat answers. Right from the original move from the Rock Church – which was so obviously a missionary act, not a breakaway act – the Fellowship has striven to act in harmony with the rest of the Church. And the missionary dimension is expressed again and again as people go out to different situations, whether in the near locality or in other parts of the country, bringing with them something of the insights of Anfield.

Chapter 10

THE WAY FORWARD

In the course of this book we have made a long journey. We have travelled from El Salvador to Liverpool, from Bombay to Colorado, from Negros to Wolverhampton.

We have felt the spirit and values of a base-community kind of Church enthusing first-world Christians as they take part in women's liturgy or in the black struggle. We have seen parishes burgeon into life, in middle-class and working-class areas alike, when they gain a local nucleus in every corner of their territory. We have paid a visit to the roughest areas of our inner cities, where Christian community work blossoms like a wild flower among the rubble. We have heard over and over again the simple, human stories of fragility and hope, of compassion and solidarity, of courage and growth.

It is time now to pull together the final ends, and for each of us to decide what is the best way forward in the context of our own life and opportunities. Each of us who reads this book with the intention of putting something into practice, at however humble a level, is a pastoral agent – a potential lump of leaven in the dough. What will be our strategy?

Is it to throw our weight into the many lively groups working for justice in imaginative ways – to share in the spirit and values of a new way of being Church without worrying whether a group is actually a basic ecclesial community or not?

Or is it to work through the parish system, in the hope of bringing the new way of being Church in the most effective way to the many ordinary, faithful Christians who deserve a better experience of Christian community?

Or is it to become inserted among the poor for whom church-going is not a way of life, so as to build Christian community right from the grassroots upwards, without the encumbrance of old expectations?

For those making the first choice, the prescription is easy: go and wherever you find the spirit and values of basic Christian community, build on that.

For those planning to start from the parish, I enclose a summary of the method that, as we have observed, has equal validity in El Salvador and London, in Negros and Colorado.

And for those planning to start from the street, I do the same, with a summary of the method that, as we have observed, has equal validity in Bombay and Wolverhampton, in Managua and Liverpool.

Starting from the parish: summary of method

1) Visiting.
The pastoral agents go out to meet the people where they live, rather than waiting in church for them to turn up there. In visiting people on their own ground – both practising Christians and others – the pastoral agents learn the religious needs that spring out of the real lives of the people. The team of pastoral agents acts like a mini-community as it engages in this action.

2) Organizing people to meet each other in their localities on the basis of a felt religious need.
When the pastoral agents have established some relationship with the church members – practising or lapsed – of a particular locality, they arrange a meeting for them in their own neighbourhood. In this way the local Christians can get to know each other and form a community. It is important to get everyone possible to this meeting, through personal invitation.

3) Ensuring that social action and religious action proceed side by side, in constant interplay.
From this first meeting onwards, life and faith are shown to be inseparably linked, so that religious practice is constantly intertwined with response to local needs, as leaking rooves are mended, the sick

are cared for, the elderly are visited, or new residents are welcomed. Scripture is read, worship held or sacraments celebrated in the local context of the new Christian community. As people get to know each other, this process becomes natural.

4) Making the local communities responsible for organizing themselves.
Though the pastoral agents have probably called together the first meeting or series of meetings, the actual organization of the local community is thrown over immediately to the people themselves. The Christian community will stand or fall by the efforts of its members.

5) Providing central, parish resources for training and support.
In-service training of those engaged in different ministries is provided at parish or deanery or diocesan level. The parish team are at the disposal of the communities – not to do things for the local Christians, but to help the local Christians do things for themselves, for example: to lead scripture discussion, to facilitate meetings, to run simple liturgical services, to organize local campaigns, and so on. Centralized resources are made available, such as office equipment, or a newsletter. The parish team also ensure that the communities are held together in a network of communication, so that local representatives meet on committees or on a parish council, and so that parish events and worship draw together the local communities as communities, rather than gathering isolated individuals.

6) Growth.
New communities grow, either from a community dividing when it becomes too big, or from people learning from the example of neighbouring communities. The structure spreads throughout the parish and into other parishes.

Starting from the street: summary of method

1) Insertion.
The pastoral agents must spend time with the people, listening to them, building up trust with them, sharing their hopes and joys, griefs and anxieties with them, before making any plans at all. This process may take months.

2) Responding to social needs.
The pastoral agents may then begin to help people organize some activity, in response to a need that has been expressed. This could be a campaign for civil rights, sport for the youth, day trips out of the area, a play group for young children, social events, etc.

3) Responding to religious needs.
In due course interest may be expressed in the faith that motivates the pastoral agents, and at this point a religious meeting or class can be started, preferably centred around a contextual reading of the Bible. Only a minority may be involved in this, and if the society is not generally a Christian one it may be a very small minority.

4) Bringing together faith and life.
Because the social needs and the religious needs have both been responded to, a context is created in which faith and life can continue to feed each other in a "pastoral cycle", or "See-Judge-Act" process. The social events will be supported by the values of sharing that come from the Christian basis; while the religious reflection will be grounded in everyday reality, rather than floating in the clouds. A more rounded form of Christian worship may now develop.

5) Maturing.
As events and procedures become established, gradually the community matures – both the wider community, and the Christian community within it. Slowly the people gain confidence, as they learn to take on responsibilities they have never had before. Regular evaluation will help people understand for themselves what works and why, and from evaluation will emerge planning. Through all

this period, the pastoral agents will be in contact with the wider Church, which will help them in their own evaluation process. This process of maturing may take five or ten years.

6) Mission.

One of the signs of maturity in a basic Christian community is that people are ready and willing to go out to others in mission. New communities may start, or individuals may go forward for training in ministry. This step into mission is one test by which we can see if a Christian community has come to a self-understanding that it is Church (whether or not it uses the language of "Church", or even the language of "basic Christian community"). Through this final step of mission, the process begins again in a new place, starting, of course, with insertion.

I will end with a true story. As a matter of fact it comes from El Salvador, but that is not important. It could equally well have happened in Britain or Australia, in Spain or Holland, in Ireland or the USA.

During a workshop given by the Marins team, each small group was given a newspaper folded into the shape of a boat, which they were told represented the Church. It was to be passed around the circle, and each person was invited in turn to re-form the newspaper model according to their idea of the Church. One refolded the newspaper into the shape of a body; another rolled it into a ball and gave it a kick; another recovered it and lovingly reshaped the boat; another drew people in the cabins; and so on. Then one person felt so angry with the Church that he took out some matches and set fire to the newspaper. It crinkled and burnt. What did he have to pass on? Only the ashes.

The last person took the ashes with great reverence. She held them in her hands, lost for a moment as to what to do with them. Then she put her thumb in the ashes and made the sign of the cross on her forehead – the traditional sign of penitence from the Ash Wednesday liturgy. She went round the group, signing each one on the forehead with the ashes. Then she told them, "There is nothing more to say. You are the Church."

NOTES

Chapter 1 (pp. 19–51)

1. *Pastoral de Conjunto*, 10.
2. *Sementes de CEBs: Grupos de Reflexão, Oração e Ação.*
3. The booklet explains that "the Reflection Groups should not be the end of our work. They should be 'seeds' and 'means' of reaching a higher objective, which is THE FORMATION OF TRUE BASIC ECCLESIAL COMMUNITIES (CEBs)."
4. Diagram from *Mission in Christ's Way: Resource Book 1990/91* (The Methodist Church Overseas Division), p. 14.
5. From *CEB – Um Jeito Novo de Ser Igreja* (Archdiocese of Goiânia, 1985). The translation of captions has been kept as literal as possible.
6. José Marins and team, *The Church from the Roots*, p. 32.
7. James O'Halloran, *Signs of Hope*, p. 11.
8. Leonardo Boff, *Ecclesiogenesis*, pp. 24–6.
9. F. Lobinger, *Building Small Christian Communities*.
10. The *plano pastoral de conjunto* (1965–70) of the Brazilian Bishops' Conference said: "Our present parishes are or should be composed of various local or 'basic' communities, because of their extension, density of population and percentage of baptized adults who by rights belong to them."
11. Pastoral Message on *The Base Ecclesial Communities, Church in Movement*, 3.6, signed at Guadalajara, Jalisco, on 7 April 1989.
12. Joe Holland and Peter Henriot, *Social Analysis: Linking Faith and Justice* (Center of Concern, 1980; rev. ed. 1983). This form of the diagram comes from the 1980 edition.
13. CAFOD stands for the Catholic Fund for Overseas Development. This diagram comes from *Proclaim Jubilee: Study Programme Leaders' Guide*, p. 5.
14. Clodovis Boff, *The Way Forward for the First World Church*, p. 8.
15. *Una Iglesia que nace del pueblo*, quoted in Pablo Galdámez, *Faith of a People*, p. 6.

16. The figure on p. 42 copies a sheet produced by Maggie Pickup for a workshop on basic Christian community. It is based on an exercise used by José Marins and team.
17. By Sally Timmel and Anne Hope, published in Zimbabwe.
18. Leonardo Boff, *Church, Charism and Power*, p. 155. Translation corrected.
19. *Ibid.*, pp. 127–8.
20. "The Journey of a People", reproduced from *Faith and Politics: The Challenge of the Christian Grassroots Communities in Brazil*, IDAC document 23/24 (Instituto de Açao Cultural, Geneva). Published by permission of IDAC.
21. Quoted in Frances O'Gorman, *Base Communities in Brazil: Dynamics of a Journey*, p. 32.
22. *CEB – um jeito novo de ser Igreja*.
23. Sally Timmel and Anne Hope, *Training for Transformation*: Book 1, p. 23.
24. "(Are you being served? A vision for a distinctive diaconate for Leicester diocese)", a report to the Board of Education and Ministry of the Diocese of Leicester, September 1990.
25. Margaret and Ian Fraser, *Wind and Fire*, p. 13.
26. *Signalement 1985: Basisbeweging van kritische groepen in gemeenten in Nederland*, pp. 1,4.
27. But there are groups in Italy that call themselves *communità ecclesiali di base* precisely in order to show that they are not *communità di base*, in the sense currently understood in Italy. This development, which is far more clergy-dominated, is unfortunately also outside the limited scope of this book.

Chapter 3 (pp. 69–82)
1. Clodovis Boff, *The Way Forward for the First World Church*, p. 8.
2. Catholic Women's Network, which organized the event.
3. Gill Sharpe, *Catholic Women's Network Newsletter*, June 1990.
4. Brid Fitzpatrick, *Catholic Women's Network Newsletter*, June 1990.
5. Catholic Association for Racial Justice.
6. This is a highly abbreviated version of the *Congress of Black Catholics – Report*, by Margaret Hebblethwaite in collaboration with Betty Luckham. Copies are available at £1.50 from Catholic Association for Racial Justice, St Vincent's Centre, Talma Road, London SW2 1AS.

Chapter 4 (pp. 83–95)
1. Maria Lopez Vigil, *Death and Life in Morazán*, p. 13.
2. *Ibid.*, pp. 15–16.
3. Pablo Galdámez, *Faith of a People*, edited from pp. 3–9.
4. Niall O'Brien, *Revolution from the Heart*, pp. 127–8.

5. *Ibid.*, pp. 198–9.
6. *Ibid.*, pp. 200–1.
7. *Ibid.*, p. 262.
8. *Ibid.*, pp. 264–5.

Chapter 5 (pp. 96–108)

1. Tony Castle is the author of *Quotes and Anecdotes for Preachers and Teachers* (Kevin Mayhew, 1979); and compiler of *The Hodder Book of Christian Quotations* (Hodder and Stoughton, 1982).
2. This is a slightly shortened version of "The Abbey Wood Experiment", from an unpublished manuscript by Tony Castle.

Chapter 6 (pp. 109–125)

1. Richard Ling's own account, "ACTION Communities", p. 2, 10 November 1989, draft chapter 2 for a forthcoming book, *Small Christian Communities: Leaven for a World Catholic Church*. Copies of the chapter obtainable from the author, price $6.00 ($7.00 overseas), at St Frances Cabrini Parish, 6673 W. Chatfield Ave., Littleton, CO 80123, USA. All quotations in this chapter come from this source and are used with the permission of the author.
2. "Pastor" in the USA is the same role as "parish priest" in Britain.
3. Address as in note 1, above.
4. Rite of Christian Initiation for Adults – a new process of welcoming adults into the Catholic Church. Its most distinctive feature is the community support given to the new member over many months.
5. See Dennis Geaney's excellent little book, *Quest for Community: Tomorrow's Parish Today*. He looks at case studies of parishes in the USA which have moved some way towards a base-community type of approach – many of them through the "Renew" programme.
6. Leonardo Boff, *Church, Charism and Power*, pp. 160, 164.

Chapter 7 (pp. 126–139)

1. The author is quoting here from the beginning of the Vatican II Pastoral Constitution, *Gaudium et Spes*: "The joys and the hopes, the griefs and the anxieties of the people of this age, especially those who are poor or in any way afflicted, these too are the joys and hopes, the griefs and anxieties of the followers of Christ." In using this quotation he is illustrating how basic Christian communities have grown out of the inspiration of Vatican II.
2. This account is taken from a longer article that appeared in *Jivan*, April 1988. The author, Paul Vaz, is the former Co-ordinator for Social Action in the Bombay Jesuit Province.

Chapter 8 (pp 140–160)

1. Poem by Carmen Brearley.
2. From Margaret Walsh, *Here's Hoping* (Urban Theology Unit, Sheffield, 1991), pp. 4–5. All quotations in this chapter come from my own taped interview with Margaret Walsh except for those with a reference to *Here's Hoping*.
3. *Ibid.*, p. 21.
4. *Ibid.*, p. 22.
5. *Ibid.*, p. 10.
6. *Ibid.*, p. 14.
7. *Ibid.*, p. 20.
8. Poem by Caroline Ann Plain.
9. Margaret Walsh, *op. cit.*, p. 8.
10. *Ibid.*, pp. 14–15.
11. *Ibid.*, p. 12.
12. *Ibid.*, pp. 20–1.

Chapter 9 (pp. 161–186)

1. Liverpool has been rated 103 out of 103 by the European Community in its proverty rating, cf. Cheshire, Carbonaro and Hay, "Problems of Urban Decline and Decay in EEC Countries" in *Urban Studies* 1986.
2. "Cave Family Prayer Letter", December 1988.
3. Roger Forster, (ed.) *Ten New Churches*, p. 77.
4. Copies of "Marginalization: A View from the Underside" can be bought from 86 Anfield Road, Liverpool L4 OTE, price £1.50.
5. Roger Forster (ed.), *op. cit,.*, p. 80.
6. The Anglican and Roman Catholic leaders, respectively.
7. In a Protestant context, "minister" customarily means "ordained minister".

BIBLIOGRAPHY

The following is a list of books, articles and pamphlets cited in the text, plus a few of the most accessible books for further reading. Addresses for obtaining some of the books are as follows: CAFOD, 2 Romero Close, Stockwell Road, London SW9 9TY; CIIR, 22 Coleman Fields, London N1 7AF; Center of Concern, 3700 13th Street N.E., Washington D.C.20017.

Anfield Road Fellowship. "Marginalisation: a View from the Underside". Report prepared for the Base Communities' Conference, Paris, 1991. Copies available from 86 Anfield Road, Liverpool L4 0TE. Price £1.50.

"Are you being served? A vision for a distinctive diaconate for Leicester diocese", 1990. Copies available from Diocese of Leicester, Church House, 3/5 St Martin's East, Leicester LE1 5FX. Price 80p.

Bambamarca, Pastoral Team of. *Vamos Caminando*. Orbis and SCM Press, 1985.

Barbé, Dominique. *Grace and Power: Base Communities and Non-violence in Brazil*. Orbis, 1987.

Boff, Clodovis. *The Way Forward for the First World Church*. CIIR, 1987.

Boff, Leonardo. *Church, Charism and Power: Liberation Theology and the Institutional Church*, Crossroad and SCM Press, 1985.

Boff, Leonardo. *Ecclesiogenesis: The Base Communities Re-invent the Church*. Orbis and Collins, 1986.

CAFOD. *Proclaim Jubilee: Study Programme Leaders' Guide*. 1986.

CAFOD. *Working Together: A Handbook for Groups*, 1986.

Catapan S.V.D., Dom Joel Ivo. *Sementes de CEBs: Grupos de Reflexão, Oração e Ação*. São Paulo, Edições Loyola, 1989.

Cave, Dave. *Jesus is your Best Mate*. Marshall Pickering, 1985.

Cave, Dave. "Anfield Road Fellowship" in *Ten New Churches*, ed. Roger Forster. Marc Europe, 1986.

CEB – Um Jeito Novo de Ser Igreja. Brazil, Archdiocese of Goiânia, 1985.

Eagleson, John and Torres, Sergio, eds. *The Challenge of Basic Christian Communities*. Orbis, 1981.

Faith and Politics: The Challenge of the Christian Grassroots Communities in Brazil. Geneva, IDAC document 23/24, Instituto de Ação Cultural.

Fitzpatrick, Brid. "Women Celebrate Death and New Life – Impressions". *Catholic Women's Network Newsletter* (June 1990).

Fraser, Ian. *Living a Countersign: From Iona to Basic Christian Communities*. Glasgow, Wild Goose Publications, 1990.

Fraser, Margaret and Ian. *Wind and Fire: The Spirit Reshapes the Church in Basic Christian Communities*. Scottish Churches House, Dunblane, Basic Communities Resource Centre, 1986.

Galdámez, Pablo. *Faith of a People*. Orbis, CIIR and Dove, 1986.

Geaney, Dennis J. *Quest for Community: Tomorrow's Parish Today*. Ave Maria Press, 1987.

Hebblethwaite, Margaret. *The Tablet* (16 April, 23 April, 30 April, 7 May 1988; 18 March, 6 May, 5 August 1989). *Alpha* (17 August 1989).

Hebblethwaite, Margaret with Luckham, Betty. *Congress of Black Catholics – Report*. CARJ, 1990. Copies available from Catholic Association for Racial Justice, St Vincent's Centre, Talma Road, London SW2 1AS. Price £1.50.

Hennelly, Alfred T., ed. *Liberation Theology: A Documentary History*, Orbis, 1990.

Holland, Joe, and Henriot, Peter. *Social Analysis: Linking Faith and Justice*. Center of Concern, 1980; rev. enl. ed. Dove, Orbis and the Center of Concern, 1983. Copies available from CAFOD.

Hope, Anne, and Timmel, Sally. *Training for Transformation: A Handbook for Community Workers*, Books 1–3. Zimbabwe, Mambo Press, 1984. Copies available from CAFOD.

Ling, Richard. "ACTION Communities", 10 November 1989, draft chapter 2 for a forthcoming book, *Small Christian Communities: Leaven for a World Catholic Church*. Copies of chapter obtainable from the author at St Frances Cabrini Parish, 6673 W. Chatfield Ave., Littleton, CO 80123, USA. Price $6.00 ($7.00 overseas).

Lobinger, F. *Building Small Christian Communities*, No. 19 M of the series *Training for Community Ministries*. Lumko Institute, 1981.

"Marginalization: a View from the Underside" see Anfield Road Fellowship.

Marins, José, Trevisan, Teolide M. and Chanona, Carolee. *The Church from the Roots*. CAFOD, 1989.

Mission in Christ's Way: Resource Book 1990/91. London, The Methodist Church Overseas Division.

O'Brien, Niall. *Revolution from the Heart*. New York, OUP; Veritas, 1987.

O'Gorman, Frances. *Base Communities in Brazil: Dynamics of a Journey*. Rio de Janeiro, Brazil, FASE-NUCLAR, 1983.

O'Halloran, James. *Living Cells: Developing Small Christian Communities*. Orbis, 1984 and rev. ed.

O'Halloran, James. *Signs of Hope: Developing Small Christian Communities*. Orbis and Columba, 1991.

Pitt, James. *Good News to All*. CIIR and CAFOD, 1980.

Proclaim Jubilee: Study Programme Leaders' Guide. CAFOD, 1986.

Sharpe, Gill. "Women's Holy Week at Harborne". *Catholic Women's Network Newsletter* (June 1990).

Sheppard, David. *Bias to the Poor*. Hodder and Stoughton, 1983.

Timmel, Sally and Hope, Anne. *Training for Transformation: A Handbook for Community Workers*, Books 1–3. Zimbabwe, Mambo Press, 1984. Copies available from CAFOD.

Training for Transformation, see Timmel, Sally and Hope, Anne.

Torres, Sergio and Eagleson, John, eds. *The Challenge of Basic Christian Communities*. Orbis, 1981.

Vamos Caminando, see Bambamarca, Pastoral Team of.

Vatican Council II: The Conciliar and post-Conciliar Documents, ed. Austin Flannery, Fowler Wright, 1975; new ed. 1981.

Vaz, Paul. "Building basic community in Bombay". *Jivan*, Rajasthan (April 1988).

Vigil, Maria Lopez. *Death and Life in Morazán*. CIIR, 1989.

Walsh, Margaret. *Here's Hoping*. 1991. Copies available from the Urban Theology Unit, 210 Abbeyfield Road, Sheffield, S4 7AZ. Price £1.50.

Walsh, Michael, and Davies, Brian. *Proclaiming Justice and Peace: One Hundred Years of Catholic Social Teaching*. CAFOD and Collins, rev. enl. ed. 1991.

Working Together: A Handbook for Groups. CAFOD, 1986.

INDEX